8—

D0961771

WHY
BE
GOOD?

WHY BE GOOD?

*Seeking Our Best Selves
in a Challenging World*

BYRON L. SHERWIN, PH.D.

Daybreak® Books
An Imprint of Rodale Books
New York, New York

Daybreak is a registered trademark of Rodale Press, Inc.

Printed in the United States of America on acid-free ∞ , recycled paper ♻

Cover Designer: Mauna Eichner
Interior Designer: Faith Hague

Library of Congress Cataloging-in-Publication Data

Sherwin, Byron L.
    Why be good? : seeking our best selves in a challenging world /
Byron L. Sherwin.
        p.   cm.
    Includes index.
    ISBN 0–87596–531–8 hardcover
    1. Ethics, Jewish.   2. Conduct of life.   I. Title.
    BJ1287.S563W59   1998
296.3'6—dc21   98–22809

Distributed in the book trade by St. Martin's Press

2 4 6 8 10 9 7 5 3 1   hardcover

—————— OUR PURPOSE ——————
*"We publish books that empower
people's minds and spirits."*

For Elliott
little brother,
great friend

Contents

Acknowledgments

My deepest gratitude to my editor, Karen Kelly, for what she has taught me during the composition of this book. My thanks to my earnest secretary Pam Spitzner for magically transforming the scrawl of my fountain pen into a presentable typescript. To Inner Traditions International, I am grateful for permission to include excerpts from my book *Crafting the Soul: Creating Your Life as a Work of Art*.

Ethical Fitness

He sees you when you're sleeping.
He knows when you're awake.
He knows if you've been bad or good,
So be good for goodness' sake.

—CHRISTMAS SONG

"Are you Santa Claus?"

An adorable little boy, six or seven years old, asked me this question as I meandered across the beach while on vacation in Florida a few years ago. He reminded me so much of my own son when he was that age that I felt myself catapulted back through the years to when my son and I would build sand castles together near the sea. And yet being mistaken for Santa Claus also reminded me that the years had passed all too quickly. My gray beard, bleached even whiter by the sun, and my expanding girth, nurtured by an overly sedentary life and a passion for food, sobered the youthful enthusiasm I had felt momentarily while lazily surveying the surf on that clear and bright morning, the day before Christmas.

"Leave the man alone, Michael," the boy's father yelled as he came running toward us. But the boy already had locked his small arms around my legs, as if he had captured a long-sought-after treasure that he was not about to let go. I thought about the biblical story of Jacob who would not let go of the angel until the angel blessed him.

The boy looked up at me and asked in rapid fire, "Are you *really* Santa Claus? Did you get the letter I sent you? Can I have a dog for Christmas?"

By this time, his father had reached us. Apologizing to me profusely, he tried to release Michael's tight but affectionate grip on my knees.

"Why do you want a dog for Christmas, Michael?" I asked the little boy.

"Because I've been good. But you're Santa. You know that already."

He began to sing the famous song that starts "You better watch out. . . ." When he came to the end, he shouted, "He knows if you've been bad or good, so be good for goodness' sake."

"Let me speak to your father for a minute, Michael," I said. "I promise I'll be right back." Michael reluctantly released his grip on my knees.

Michael's father clumsily apologized again, not quite knowing what to say.

"Are you planning to get Michael a dog for Christmas?" I asked him.

"Yes, as soon as we get home from vacation."

"Is it because he has been a good boy?"

"Yes, he has," the father said sheepishly.

"Can I tell him?" I asked.

"Sure," said Michael's father, relieved.

I went over to Michael, whose eyes shone with nervous anticipation. I knelt in front of him, my hands on his shoulders, my eyes looking into his. I smiled.

"Michael," I asked, "have you been 'good for goodness' sake'?"

"I don't know," he responded.

"Well, I know that you have been a good boy this past year. Do you promise to continue to be a good boy?"

"Sure," he said, kicking the sand with his small foot.

"Then, as soon as you get back home after your visit here in Florida, you are going to get a wonderful dog. You have *my* word on it. But you must love this dog and take good care of it."

His face lit up like a Christmas tree.

"Thank you, thank you, Santa," he said, reaching up to give me a hug.

"Now, you just remember to be a good boy like you promised," I said, turning to resume my walk. Michael returned to his digging. His father, however, ran after me.

"Thanks. Thanks a lot, mister," he said. "My son's too young to give up believing in Santa Claus. This will always be a very special Christmas for him because he believes that he really met Santa Claus."

"I'm glad, too," I said. "But it's all very strange."

"Why?" he asked.

"Because I could never believe in Santa Claus myself," I said.

"Why's that?"

"Because I'm Jewish. Actually, I'm a rabbi."

"Well, anyway, thanks again for what you did for my boy. But if Jesus could be a Jew, why can't Santa Claus?" he said, and walked away.

I continued my walk along the beach, thinking about what had just happened. Though this was the first time I had been mistaken for Santa Claus, it was not likely to be the last—unless I went on a diet and dyed my beard. But it was not the first time I had discussed with someone whether they had been "good for goodness' sake." In the more than a quarter of a century since I had been ordained a rabbi, and in more than 30 years as a teacher, I have had countless conversations with people of all ages and backgrounds about whether they were good, about whether they had acted morally, about whether they had chosen or were about to choose the right thing to do. Here is how some of these conversations began.

"My father is in a coma. The doctors don't expect him to recover consciousness. Medical insurance is running out. Bills are piling up. The hospital tells me that the decision is mine—not theirs, not the doctor's—that it's a moral, not a medical, decision. Should I have my father removed from the respirator and allow him to die?"

"One of my co-workers is stealing from the company. Not a lot—a few dollars from petty cash here and there, some office supplies now and then—but if every employee did it, it would cost the company a fortune. This co-worker is also my friend. Should I blow the whistle on her? I owe it to the company to do that—but then I'll lose a friend and get the reputation of being a snitch."

"Everybody cheats in my high school class. If I don't cheat, too, I'll be at a comparative disadvantage. After all, everybody's doing it; why shouldn't I do it, too? Why should I be penalized for being honest?"

"We didn't know why my wife wasn't conceiving a child, so we began infertility treatments. It's been a depressing and humiliating experience—with no results, except that I found out I'm almost sterile. After a lot of soul-searching, we've decided that if we can't have a child genetically related to both of us, we should have one related to one of us, to my wife. What do you think about donor artificial insemination? Is it the right thing for us to do?"

"I know that my teenage daughter is sexually active, and that she rarely uses contraceptive or protective measures. Should I provide her with prophylactics, and should I ask our doctor to either prescribe birth control pills or have her fit for a diaphragm? I don't approve of what she's doing, but I don't want her to get into trouble."

"I know the Bible says that we should honor and respect our parents. But my father is a rotten guy. He cheats in business to get by. He exploits and manipulates people. Am I obliged to respect and honor him just because he's my father?"

"My best friend is becoming an alcoholic. Should I talk to him about it? His wife tried and he walked out of the house and didn't return all night. Sometimes he gets violent when people kid him about it. Should I be a good friend and confront him about it—even though it might destroy our 20-year-long friendship?"

"I went to a conference in Paris. It was my first time there. It was also the first time in 16 years of marriage that I slept with someone other than my husband. It just happened. There he was. There I was. Both of us had had too much to drink. The atmosphere was conducive. Paris is so romantic. He was handsome. I was lonely. Now, I'm pregnant, in the eighth week. If I confess to my husband, he might divorce me. Either way, things would never be the same between us. We have two children. My lover is also married with children. Should I tell him? Should I tell my husband? Should I have an abortion? I'm going nuts."

When my brother was in grade school, he had to write his first essay. He decided to write about biology. The first sentences read, "Biology is everywhere. You can't get rid of it." The same is true of ethics. Ethical problems and issues are everywhere. You can't get rid of them. Just read through a daily newspaper or a weekly newsmagazine and count how many articles relate to moral problems, either in the individual, local, national, or international arenas.

Ethics is a vital and inextricable part of the art of living. Who we are and who we aspire to become are, to a significant degree, the result of the decisions we make—and many of those decisions are ethical. From time to time, it is worth pausing to reflect upon the conscious choices we have made and how they have shaped our lives. Choices about education, career, marriage, family re-lationships, friendships, and finances all express values and com-mitments that we held at the time we made them. Some we may find we regret, while others we continue to embrace as being central to our lives.

We are constantly composing the story of our lives by the choices we make and by the ethical convictions and values that underlie them. These values serve as a barometer to help us un-derstand how successful we have been in the quest to be moral and good. Our choice of moral values sets precedents for our fu-ture choices and often determines what we will decide to do in a moment of crisis and serious moral choice.

While scientific knowledge and technological skill have de-veloped far beyond that of yesteryear, thus rendering past theo-ries and technologies obsolete, this has not been the case as far as spiritual and moral wisdom is concerned. We have, for example, witnessed startling advances in modern medical science. Every year, there are more and more breathtaking developments in health care. People are generally healthier, and they live longer than in times past. But are people morally better? Has the quality of our spiritual and moral health improved in the same way that the quality of our physical existence has been enhanced? We know more and we can do more to achieve physical health than in cen-turies past. But are we able to do more to enhance our moral lives than our ancestors were able to do?

You may come from a family where ethical values were nur-tured and taught. You may have been raised among honest, hard-working people. You may have been taught great moral truths in church, synagogue, or mosque. You may have received high grades in courses in ethics at a college or university. You may have worked with a group of dedicated people with high integrity, a sense of fairness, and mutual respect. You may have a loving and caring spouse and children. All of these things are conducive to making you an ethical person. But, in the final analysis, whether you are a good person ultimately depends on you.

Precisely because ethical decisions are so much a part of our lives, it is important for each of us to be and to remain ethically fit. Should a weighty moral decision suddenly confront us, we must be prepared to engage it. Being ethically fit is no less important than being physically fit. Like physical fitness, ethical fitness requires effort to be attained and maintained. It is not acquired genetically, nor by osmosis. Let it slip away, and it becomes increasingly difficult to retrieve. It does not come through an intensive quick fix but by sustained perseverance. Just as a bird must continue flapping its wings in order to fly, ethical fitness requires constant attention and commitment. It demands an ongoing engagement of intellect, emotion, intuition, will, thought, and action.

What if there were a health club for the purpose of helping us keep spiritually and morally fit? What would an ethical workout entail? At our local gym, we might get on a treadmill and walk or run for a certain number of minutes or miles. But at a moral health club, there might be an exercise that would have us step off the treadmill of our daily routine to provide us with quiet time to contemplate where we are going in life. Such an exercise would offer us the opportunity to define and adjust our priorities in life to our moral values and convictions. It would give us a chance to ask ourselves whether the daily treadmill we find ourselves on really leads anywhere. Does it bring us to where and to whom we want to be?

Part of a physical workout is often lifting weights. But a moral workout would do precisely the opposite. It would ask us to consider whether the pressures upon us and within us are already too heavy for us to bear, whether the weights of our daily obligations are the right ones or not, whether they are compatible with our moral values and commitments, and if they match our true priorities in life.

Some people lift weights that are not really there. Maybe you know such people. They like to fabricate things to worry about. They are like the old joke: "What is a Jewish telegram? One that reads: Start worrying now, details to follow." Rather than concentrating on what really matters, rather than attending to being morally and spiritually fit, they become obsessed with insignificant things. They may worry about unlikely catastrophes that they feel certain will befall them or someone they know. As a result, their lives are in danger of becoming a game of trivial pursuit.

Various physical exercises aim at strengthening different muscle groups, while others purport to aid in removing harmful toxins from the body. An ethical workout would focus on strengthening different moral virtues, particularly those that might be weak. One exercise could elevate our capacity for friendship. One could intensify our power to love. Another could invigorate our attitude of gratitude. Still another could strengthen our ability to manage our ego. Finally, there could be ethical exercises that would aim to dispel certain moral vices like greed, arrogance, hatred, and obsessive anger.

At health clubs, people often hire a personal trainer to plan a health regimen for them. What kind of trainer would a moral health club seek to engage? What kind of trainer could help you keep ethically fit? What kinds of training and knowledge would such a person be expected to have?

An ethical trainer—a person competent to guide moral fitness—is called an ethicist. Such an individual is conversant with the accumulated wisdom of the past, has mastered a variety of methodologies in ethical decision making, and is adept at applying that wisdom and in applying those methodologies to the moral problems that we confront on a daily basis. Just as we would lack confidence in a sickly physician with bad health habits, so would we question the competence of an ethicist who is not a good person.

The experienced physician treats his patients not only on the basis of a knowledge of anatomy and pathology learned in medical school but also on the basis of having treated many patients with certain symptoms and diseases. The knowledge and experience of the seasoned physician is brought to bear in the treatment of each patient. Similarly, the ethicist who has spent many years studying, thinking about, and applying the wisdom of the past to the moral problems of the present does not address a moral problem from the perspective of his personal opinion or feeling at a given time. Rather, the ethicist applies the experiences and insights of thousands of people over hundreds of years to the problem at hand. The ethicist uses methods of analysis honed throughout generations of dealing with moral problems, and to these he adds his own insight in applying acquired knowledge and methodological skills to the problem.

We would not consult a person untrained in medicine for a medical problem. We would not hire a person who is not a licensed attorney to represent us in a legal matter. Yet we rely on a wide variety of individuals with no particular knowledge of the moral or spiritual wisdom of the past, and with no training in the application of methodologies in ethical decision making, to shape our moral attitudes and actions.

For example, is a media celebrity or a leading sports figure the appropriate person from whom to seek spiritual and moral guidance? Are talk-show hosts and hostesses the best qualified individuals to be our ethical trainers? Can a sound bite on a talk show provide a penetrating in-depth analysis of a complex moral problem? Most of us would answer no to these questions. Nonetheless, every day millions of people tune in to radio and TV programs to find guidance about how to lead their lives.

While not all shows are the same, and while some are surely better than others, they seem inadequate to deal competently with the ethical issues they often address. On some shows, the goal seems to be making people *feel* good rather than *be* good. The aim seems to be to give people permission to do all kinds of outlandish things. "Are you going to tell us how you hacked into your school computer, changed all your grades, and were awarded a scholarship to an Ivy League Law School?" "Do you enjoy your work as a male prostitute?—Oh, I'm not a male prostitute, I'm a professional sex provider." "When you were a little boy, did you think you'd grow up to be a 'hit man'?"

Other talk shows I have seen and heard do the exact opposite. They provide a forum for people who want to be yelled at, castigated, or humiliated for things they were doing that either are or might be wrong. On many of these shows, people with little background in the topic they're discussing spout moral guidance, advice, and admonitions. No one would put a scalpel in their hands to perform a surgical operation. Why then do so many people turn to them for moral guidance?

Historically, clergy have served as ethical trainers, and many members of the clergy have been trained as ethicists. For this reason, it is appropriate to seek the advice of clergy in ethical decision making. Clergy are trained to be able to help people think through moral problems within the context of the religious tradition that they represent. However, sometimes people come to clergy for the same reasons that they watch and participate in certain talk shows—or, at least, to get something off their chest so that they can *feel* better even if they do not want to *be* better.

There are still others who try to undermine and corrupt the clergyperson in order to show themselves that the clergyperson is just as corruptible as they are. For example, a young woman once came to see me to talk about her sexual promiscuity. After describing in the most vivid detail a long line of indiscriminate sexual liaisons she had had, she stood up, fell into my lap, started caressing me, and asked, "Is sleeping with a rabbi a religious experience?" She wanted to seduce me to justify her previous behavior by showing me that I would act as she had done if given the opportunity. I was sorry to have had to disappoint her. Further, a man once came to talk about how he unscrupulously manipulated his business affairs by buying people off, and then he dangled a substantial donation to my favorite charity in front of me to demonstrate that since I play the same game, he should not be held morally culpable for his wrongs. Unfortunately, I had to disappoint him, too.

Just as medical opinions and diagnoses may differ with regard to the same case, so the views of ethicists sometimes differ on the matters brought before them. Ethicists can provide us with a range of informed choices and moral prescriptions. But they cannot make ethical decisions for us. Just as a physical trainer can recommend an exercise regimen for us, and just as a physician can prescribe for us a program of treatment or a health regimen, so an ethicist can offer us guidance about ethical living and decision making. However, he cannot make us good. He cannot make ethical decisions for us that will shape the kind of person each of us would like to be. Ultimately, it is the individual who must make and take responsibility for his own decisions and actions. Being good is a challenge and a task confronting each of us. But how do we go about it? How do we gain and maintain ethical fitness?

⤫

The rabbi of Rhyzen once entered a room where he found his closest disciples playing checkers. When the students saw their master, they were deeply embarrassed, for they knew they should have been studying sacred texts rather than squandering their time playing games. But the rabbi of Rhyzen was not angry. He approached his disciples and said, "I am glad that you are playing checkers, for if you have learned the rules of checkers, then you have learned something important about spiritual and moral development, about ethical fitness. There are three rules in checkers that are also three rules for spiritual and moral development. First, you should move one step at a time. Don't skip steps. Second, you should move only forward, and not backward. Finally, when you have reached the highest rung, you can move whichever way you want."

How to Be Good

*L*ike the boy I met on the beach, Calvin in the cartoon above has to decide between being good or doing something bad that might hurt his chances of getting a reward from Santa. In deciding whether to hit Susie with a snowball, Calvin is confronted with a right versus wrong decision.

In right versus wrong decisions, we usually know what is right and what is not. The choice is whether or not we want to do what is right. There are also right versus right decisions, however, and they often offer tougher choices than right versus wrong decisions. For example:

> It is right to alleviate the pain of a dying patient, but it is also right to extend life as long as possible. What if

13

administering a painkilling drug might also kill the patient?

It is right for a woman to make decisions affecting her body. It is also right for an unborn child to be born. What if a woman is deciding whether or not to have an abortion?

It is right for a family to take a much-needed vacation and to spend quality time together. It is also right for parents to save money for their children's education. What should parents decide to do when money is limited?

It is right for artists to be able to express themselves freely. It is also right for the community to prohibit the public display of offensive and pornographic materials. Should an artist's right to free expression be restricted, and if so, under what conditions?

It is right to reward conscientious workers with a merit pay raise. But, in a financially unstable company, it is also right to contain costs to protect the fiscal stability of the company. Should management accrue debt by financially rewarding its workers? Should certain workers be discharged to permit the company to give higher compensation to those considered to be more vital to the company?

Whether in issues of right versus right or right versus wrong, making moral decisions is not easy. One factor in making moral decisions is intention. If the intention of the person acting is good, then the action may be moral. If the intention of the person is bad, then the action may be immoral.

A masked stranger has you put on a table. One of his associates drugs you into unconsciousness. He takes out a sharp knife and slices into your body.

Is this act moral, immoral, or amoral? It depends on the intention and the situation.

If the masked stranger is an enemy of yours who has kidnapped you in order to torture, mutilate, and kill you, the act is clearly immoral. But if the masked stranger is a surgeon trying to save your life in an emergency operation after an automobile crash, then it is moral.

> A man pushes a woman down on a bed, rips her clothes off, and has sexual intercourse with her.

Is this act immoral, moral, or amoral? If he is a rapist and she is his victim, then it's immoral. If they are lovers, and a moment before entering the bedroom, she said to him, "When we get into the bedroom, I want you to rip off my clothes and have sex with me," then it may be amoral, moral, or immoral. If she is the teenage babysitter, then it is probably immoral. If she is his wife, then it is probably moral. If one of them is HIV-positive but has kept that fact from the other, then it is immoral. It all has to do with intentions as well as with the nature of the relationship, possible outcomes, and agreements between the parties. It is not always the nature of an act in itself that determines whether it is moral, amoral, or immoral. Intention and situation are often key factors.

In many cases, intention is the determining factor of whether an action is moral or not. But in other cases, we must look beyond intention. As the old quip puts it, "The road to hell is paved with good intentions." Sometimes an act can be done with the most noble of intentions, but it can still be wrong. For instance, if a person commits a spree of robberies in order to feed the poor, the intention is good, but the act is inherently immoral, despite the outcome. Even people who might consider the activities of the thief as being moral would surely change their minds once they found themselves the victims of his robberies.

What about a good deed with expected good outcomes, but motivated by bad intentions? For example, a famous mafioso once made a charitable gift to a hospital with the explicit intention of wanting to alter his public image while he was on trial for heinous crimes. Presumably, he hoped this would mitigate the sentence if he were found guilty. The results of this action would help many people. Nonetheless, his action might not be considered moral because his intentions and motivations were manipulative and self-serving. Whether it is moral for the hospital to accept the gift is another question altogether.

There is an approach to ethical decision making, known as Utilitarianism, that might consider the thief's robberies aimed at feeding the poor and the mafioso's gift to the hospital to be moral actions. Utilitarianism focuses on the outcome of an action rather than upon its intention. Put crudely, Utilitarianism proposes that moral action is governed by the maxim: Do whatever produces the greatest good for the greatest number of people. At the heart of this approach is a "cost-benefit" approximation of the consequences of an action. The primary consideration is not whether an act is intrinsically good or bad, or whether a certain moral rule ought to be followed or not, but what the results of an action are expected to be. From this perspective, an action is done with the right intention if it aims at bringing good to the largest number of people possible. Though many people are unaware of it, they are utilitarians. They tend to make a wide variety of personal, business, and moral decisions on a kind of "cost-benefit" analysis basis. But there are numerous difficulties with this approach.

Utilitarianism is often described as a pragmatic approach. But there is always the danger of confusing the expedient with the pragmatic. What may seem in the short term to produce the best results for the most people may, in the long run, produce less than desirable results for the majority of people affected. Historical experience has demonstrated that human beings are not very good prognosticators of the long-term effects of their actions. What seems to be a good idea at a particular time can prove to be catastrophic in the long run. The future has too many unknowns. What appears to be immediately beneficial can easily degenerate into a disaster. Consider, for example, Nazi Germany.

At first, Hitler's rise to power seemed to benefit the majority of Germans. The economy improved dramatically. The German currency, devalued by runaway inflation, was stabilized. Millions of unemployed people were given jobs. The national humiliation of the Versailles Treaty was replaced with a new national pride and self-confidence. Yet, in the long run, what were the results? The devastation of a world war and the systematic murder of millions of innocent people during the Holocaust. What seemed to be beneficial to the majority of German citizens led to members of minority groups in Germany, such as German Jews, being stripped of their rights and citizenship. Many were sent to concentration camps where they were dehumanized. Many more were sent to death camps where they were starved, beaten, and murdered. All of this was done in the name of bringing benefits to the majority of people in Germany at a certain point in history.

Another example is the use of fluorocarbons in spray cans and chemicals like freon in air conditioners. Though they were originally intended to provide comfort and convenience to millions of people, the unpredicted result was the depletion of our ozone layer, which threatens all of us with the effects of harmful solar radiation.

Unbeknownst to himself, Michael—the boy I met on the beach—embraced an outcomes-oriented view of ethics. Despite his song about being "good for goodness' sake," he didn't really want to be good for the sake of being good. He didn't consider doing the ethical thing as intrinsically good. Rather, he was motivated by the expected outcomes of being good. He wanted to be good because the chance of getting a puppy would be greater.

Since biblical times, people have been warned to choose to be good and consequently to receive certain rewards, and not to be bad, thereby averting certain punishments. In this "carrot and stick" approach to ethics, God is portrayed as a kind of celestial bookkeeper with a huge accounting ledger. Each of us has a page where our credits (our good deeds) and where our debits (our bad deeds) are recorded. Our good deeds earn us "goodies," while our bad deeds bring upon us punishments and travails.

Both personally and theologically, I find this approach problematic. God, it seems to me, has more important things to do than to keep a celestial balance sheet on each of our deeds up to date. God somehow seems less godly to me when conceived as an accountant (no offense to accountants intended). I prefer to conceive of God as a loving, creative being, rather than as an obsessive, rigid numbers-cruncher, preoccupied with tallies and with bottom lines on a balance sheet. Yet many people view both God and life in this way. They think about their parents, children, friends, and colleagues as if they were accountants, always in the midst of an audit of their personal account, of their individual deeds. Such people live in a constant state of anxiety and guilt—anxiety that their account is running at a deficit, guilty that they have not amassed enough credits to avoid inevitable punishment, disapproval, and eventual rejection.

This, I believe, is an incorrect view of God, of life, and of religion. It is an idea that causes misery to many people and actually stifles their moral and spiritual development. Focusing only on the balance sheet, this view denudes God and us of love and compassion. It makes us less, rather than more, human. It stifles our spontaneity and flexibility. It eclipses the great religious insight that God loves us even if we make mistakes.

It is hard enough to be good, yet many people think that they have to be better than good, that they have to be perfect. This is not only an unrealistic idea but a dangerous one as well. Human beings are, by nature, imperfect. No one can ever fulfill the expectation of being perfect, and people who believe that they can only set themselves up for a life of frustration and anxiety. And, once people realize that they cannot be perfect, they might simply give up and relent in the quest to be virtuous.

A business executive in California has a sign on his desk that reads: "Babe Ruth struck out 1,330 times." Failure is the flip side of success. Our achievements only become meaningful when seen against the backdrop of our actual and potential failures. No one hits a home run every time in baseball, nor would anyone expect to do so. If a batter fails 60 percent of the time but succeeds 40 percent of the time and bats .400, he is an enormous success.

Expecting perfection is illusionary. Yet many people live their lives in anxiety and frustration because they fear not being perfect—not being in perfect health, not being perfect spouses, children, colleagues, friends, and so on.

For people who are obsessed with perfection, making a mistake is an irreparable catastrophe that they expect will inevitably call down the wrath of others upon them. Yet making a mistake can become an opportunity for learning something new, for moral development, and for discovering the healing power of forgiveness and love. No one would punish a child learning how to walk because the child stumbles and falls. Yet some people berate themselves as they go through life. They fail to realize that their existence is not fixed, but ever changing and moving. Being perfect is not part of our nature, but being able to learn from and correct our mistakes is. That's why pencils still have two sides, lead and an eraser. The horror of not achieving perfection can inhibit our actions, paralyze our talents, and stifle our quest for virtuous living.

Another difficulty with the "accounting ledger" view is that it contradicts the nature of the universe and of our own life experience. Neither God nor the universe is a celestial vending machine into which we deposit good deeds and consequently collect inevitable rewards. The often-heard refrain "it's not fair" is another way of saying that people feel that they are not getting their just desserts. But expecting life always to treat us fairly is as unrealistic as expecting perfection of ourselves and others. As a wise man once told me, "Expecting life to be fair because you are good is like expecting an angry bull not to charge at you because you are a vegetarian."

We may believe that "crime doesn't pay," yet we see that crime sometimes does pay, and that it pays very well. So why not commit a crime? While virtue and vice do not always bring their expected results, they often do. For example, sooner or later gluttony brings about obesity, and often other diseases as well. Avarice and greed may bring certain rewards, but there are other prices—such as those learned by Scrooge—that such behavior often dearly costs us. Were we to cast away all notions of moral propriety just because reward and punishment are not meted out with scientific precision, society would become a dysfunctional anarchy, devoid of any stability or meaning. Without a moral fiber holding it together, a society will unravel with catastrophic results.

Some people need the expectation of reward or punishment to motivate them to do certain things and to relent from doing other things. Children, for example, often need to be conditioned to certain behavioral patterns by the promise of reward and the threat of punishment. It takes time for them to develop a moral sense and to appreciate that virtue is its own reward.

The more developed a person's moral sense becomes, the less he depends on the expectation of reward or punishment as the prime motivation for his behavior. While the expectation of reward and the threat of punishment may continue to function as motivating factors for certain types of behavior, they cannot serve as *the* motivating factors for desired behavior. In the final analysis, the motivation for moral behavior must come from within. Perhaps this is one of the things Jesus meant when he said, "The kingdom of heaven is within."

Animals as well as people can be trained to act in a certain way, but is this moral behavior or simply a conditioned response motivated by promises or threats of pleasure or pain, of approval or disapproval? Is a conditioned response a morally good act? Is a dog's action, based on fear of punishment or expectation of reward, a moral action? Is a person's action any different? If we strive to be good primarily for the expected rewards it may bring and for the travails it may mitigate, is it being good that we pursue, or is it the reward for being good that primarily motivates our actions? If a child does his chores in order to get a promised new toy, are the child's actions morally good, or are they the fulfillment of a contract to receive a payoff? If an adult is primarily motivated not to steal office supplies from the workplace by the fear of being fired, is this moral behavior or is it amoral behavior motivated by the fear of being caught and punished?

If outcomes and intentions cannot always completely determine whether or not an act is moral, what about focusing on the action itself? What about following the rules? Theologically, a rule-based morality requires a person to obey the religious commandments—at all times, without exception. For instance, the biblical commandment "Thou shalt not steal" means that whatever your intentions or feelings, whatever the situation or outcome, don't steal from anyone at any time. Philosophically, rule-based morality is usually identified with the eighteenth-century German philosopher Immanuel Kant and what he called the categorical imperative (a fancy term with which to impress your friends at parties). An example offered by Kant is to never lie, because once you tell a lie, you become a liar. According to Kant, moral rules are universal, which means that they apply to all people in all conceivable situations. In other words, there are no exceptions to the rules.

The advantage of a rule-based morality is that it helps us define what is right and what is wrong. It offers us direction and guidance. Rather than each person having to invent rules and guidelines from scratch for a wide variety of situations where an ethical decision needs to be made, a rule-ethic gives us answers to how to behave in a wide variety of situations. When we are confronted with a difficult ethical choice, often at a time of psychological stress, having clear rules available is comforting and beneficial.

Living in a society where people know the rules of expected behavior is like playing a game where everyone knows the rules and tacitly agrees to obey them. If we were to play a game without rules, or if we had to make the rules up as we went along, we would have to stop the game each time a new situation arose and debate what rule to establish. Playing a game without rules eventually becomes chaotic. Similarly, a society without rules, or a society where each person makes his own rules, would lead to ethical anarchy and would inevitably unravel and collapse.

Despite its obvious advantages, a rule-based morality also has certain clear disadvantages. For instance, to demand blind adherence

to universal moral rules overlooks the realities of human individualism and the existence of unique circumstances in an imperfect
world. Few moral rules can be applied by all people, at all times, in
all situations. There must sometimes be exceptions to rules.

Having absolute, unbreakable rules invites unnecessary
rigidity when we are confronted with particular situations. We
need wisdom to determine when a rule should be set aside. In
certain situations, following the rules can have destructive moral
and social consequences. This is certainly true if a rule is silly, irrelevant, or harmful. Yet it can even be true if a rule is thoughtful,
valid, and generally beneficial but not pertinent to the particular
situation at hand.

The Talmudic rabbis realized that an absolute rule-ethic is problematic. They tell us that God wants us to be good, to do good, to
strive for piety, but that God also wants us to be wise. Being wise
means knowing when to follow the rules and when to make an exception to the rules. A person who always follows the rules to the
letter may be obedient and may do his duty. But such a person may
also be doing something that is neither wise nor good.

To illustrate this insight, the Talmud speaks about a "pious
fool," that is, a person who does stupid things with bad effects
while obeying the rules. The Talmud tells of a young man who
has been taught a rule forbidding a man to look at a nude
woman to whom he is not married. This young man is on his
way home. He comes to a pond. A nude woman is drowning in
the pond and is screaming for someone to rescue her. The
young man surveys the situation and decides that since it is forbidden for him to look at her, he should not attempt to save her,
and he lets her drown.

Kant taught that a person should obey the rule to always tell
the truth no matter what. But what if telling the truth would lead
to the death or harm of another person? Is following the rules
without exception, is telling the truth no matter what, more precious than a human life, more important than kindness or loyalty?

Suppose a mother is called to pick up her daughter who has
taken ill at school. She is worried about leaving her four-year-old

son alone in the house, even though she expects to return within 10 minutes. Before she leaves, she says to him, "Now, Tony, stay in your room, and don't leave it for any reason until I get back." When she returns, she finds that Tony has wet his pants. "Why didn't you go to the bathroom?" she asks. "Because you told me not to leave my room until you got back," he replies.

Another problem with an absolute rule-ethic is that it can make people morally lazy. It can lead us to neglect our ethical exercise. When we rely on the rules, and only on the rules, we are in danger of morally disenfranchising ourselves from the ethical decision-making process. Rules are there to help guide us in making decisions, rather than to make those decisions for us. We should think about the rules as they relate to a specific situation rather than allow the rules to think for us. Every day, we see examples of people who fall back on obviously irrelevant or inappropriate rules or policies simply because it is easier than risking initiative, exercising the mind, assuming responsibility, or making the effort to employ common sense.

No matter how many rules there are, and no matter how good they may be, there never can be enough rules to cover every possible situation. Even if there were, it would take a lifetime to know them all. Despite the presence of rules, each of us is inevitably confronted with certain situations that require us to make independent moral judgments and decisions. Moreover, even if we would know all the rules, we must be able to interpret their meaning as well as their application to particular situations. By their very nature, rules require interpretation, and interpretations tend to vary and even to conflict with one another. Yet without interpretation, rules are meaningless. Rules offer guidance, but they can't serve as substitutes to the ethical decision-making process.

A final problem with a rule-ethic is what may be called the loophole mentality. While ethical rules are usually established to encourage moral behavior, the loophole mentality tries to find ways to subvert the rules and to manipulate them for a person's own ends.

I once spoke to a law school professor who taught "Legal Ethics," a course required by most American law schools. The focus of this course is the legal profession's code of ethics.

"My goal in teaching this course," he said, "is to imbue in future lawyers a value system that will enable them to maintain their professional integrity and to further the cause of justice. But my students see it differently. The best ones see this as an 'easy A' course. However, most of my students are interested in studying the professional code of ethics to learn how to circumvent its rules, how to escape being caught for violating its requirements, and what to do to escape punishment if they are caught violating it."

He then went on to tell me about a case that came before a disciplinary review board for local attorneys. A certain lawyer had been handling a divorce case for an attractive female client. He had initiated a sexual affair with this particularly vulnerable woman—and then billed her for the time he spent in bed with her for "professional services rendered." Fortunately, his license to practice law was suspended.

Because having many rules can be confusing, a variety of religious traditions have attempted to locate a single rule that can govern moral behavior, a basic rule from which all of ethical decision making can flow. This single rule is popularly known as the Golden Rule: Do unto others what you would like them to do unto you. Variations of this rule are found in the New Testament, the Talmud, and the teachings of Confucius, Aristotle, the Koran, and elsewhere. Philosophers call this approach reversibility. In other words, put yourself in someone else's shoes and imagine how you would feel if you were the recipient, rather than the performer, of your actions.

The Golden Rule is rooted in empathy, which asks us to consider ourselves as the object rather than as the agent of our actions. It assumes self-awareness—that we know ourselves well enough to know how we would feel in a certain situation. It also assumes self-transcendence—that we can focus on someone else's feelings and conditions rather than only on our own. And it assumes action—*doing* unto others.

The Talmudic rabbis tell a beautiful story to illustrate the Golden Rule. This story explains why the Holy Temple in Jerusalem was built where it once stood.

Once there were two brothers who loved one another very much. The younger brother had a wife and four children. The older brother never married, and he lived alone. The brothers were poor farmers who each worked very hard and eked out a living on the field that their father had bequeathed equally to them. Each year at harvest time, they divided the produce. Each took his share and stacked it outside of his own house.

Once, the older brother awoke in the middle of the night and was troubled. "How unfair of me to take half of the harvest," he said to himself. "My brother has a wife and children to feed. I should give my brother a larger share of the harvest."

So, in the middle of the night, the older brother secretly carried part of his share of the harvest to his brother's house. He placed it outside of the house, adding to what his brother already had stacked there.

Meanwhile, the younger brother also awoke from his sleep troubled. "All these years, I have been equally dividing the harvest work with my brother," he said to himself. "But I have been unfair. I have a wife and children to give me comfort, but he is alone. When I am old, my children will help take care of me. But he will be alone, with no one to support him."

So, in the middle of the night, the younger brother carried part of his share of the harvest and deposited it outside of his brother's house with his brother's share of the harvest.

Neither of the brothers knew what the other was doing, so each was amazed that despite his efforts to give part of his own share of the harvest to the other, his own share never seemed to be depleted. So each man continued to bring part of his share of the harvest to his brother during the night, constantly increasing the amount, and always being surprised that his own share never seemed to be diminished.

Finally, one night, the two brothers met. Each quickly understood what the other was doing. They embraced, kissed, and wept in love and joy.

When God saw this, He decided to have the Holy Temple built on the exact spot where the brothers met that night.

⌁

Empathy is at the root of moral relations because it moves people to articulate moral values through their deeds. It opens up a door to sharing the joys and pain of others. It helps to establish and to strengthen mutual understanding and interpersonal relationships. Empathy is a key ingredient in the most cherished of all interpersonal relationships: love.

What apathetic people lack is empathy. What people who commit the most heinous of crimes are devoid of is empathy. Their inability to feel their victim's pain allows them to tell themselves lies that encourage their crime. For example, rapists may convince themselves that "she really wants it." Child abusers persuade themselves that they're not hurting anyone, that they're only providing discipline.

While attractive at first blush, the Golden Rule poses a number of problems. For example, is it workable? Do people really know how they would feel in someone else's shoes? Do they know themselves well enough, and do they know the other person well enough, to do so? How can people know how they would feel in a situation that is outside the range of their own experiences? For example, I once was walking down the street with a colleague. He went over to a homeless person begging for money in front of an office building, gave him some money, and said, "I know how you feel." The homeless person looked him over and said, "Thanks, but I doubt it."

Obeying the Golden Rule presumes abilities for attentive listening to another person, developed virtues of compassion and altruism, and, of course, empathy. While these are desirable, they are not found in abundance. People often have little time for listening to all but a few other people. Trying to be compassionate and empathetic to everyone is beyond anyone's capacity. For example, in volunteer charitable organizations, we increasingly hear about "compassion fatigue." Faced with so many people in need, we tend to tune out rather than be overwhelmed. Like many examples of excess, too much empathy can prove to be counterproductive. It can smother the ability of the other person to act on his own. It can infantilize him and stunt his own moral development. Furthermore, the Golden Rule, after all, is still a variety of a rule-ethic, with all the drawbacks and advantages that a rule-ethic has.

Of the various versions of the Golden Rule, I prefer the interpretation found in Judaism (and Confucianism) the best. Not because I'm Jewish, but simply because I have read all the versions and I think it's the best one. It says: Do *not* do unto others what you would *not* want them to do unto you. Here, we are asked to consider those things that we find most morally abhorrent and to restrain ourselves from ever doing them to another individual. The other version, "Do unto others," sounds to me too much like a preemptive military strike: Do it to them before they do it to you. As union boss Jimmy Hoffa once said, "I do it to them before they do it to me—only worse."

Each of these three approaches—Utilitarianism, the rule-ethic, and the Golden Rule—has both advantages and problems. But using a combination of their teachings in the process of deciding how to be good can help us to become morally fit. Utilitarianism reminds us to be attentive to the possible results of our actions. It asks us to remain aware of the fact that our actions have consequences and effects. Though we cannot always predict what all of them may be, we must remain aware of the fact that even the best intended acts, that even following moral norms, might lead to ethically and socially undesirable results. The rule-ethic provides us with moral norms and offers us rules by which to act morally. Though there may be exceptions to these rules, we need moral principles in order to be able to distinguish between right and wrong. Following the Golden Rule reminds us that most moral deeds involve other people, not only ourselves. Despite its drawbacks, the Golden Rule does encourage us to cultivate certain moral virtues such as empathy, compassion, and love. The Golden Rule reminds us that where ethics is concerned, no one is an island. We are interdependent.

Once there was a group of people in a boat. Suddenly, one person took out a drill and started to make a hole underneath his seat with it. The water began to come into the boat. The others admonished him, "What are you doing? You will sink the boat." The man replied, "What concern is it of yours? I am only drilling under my own seat."

✥ 3 ✥

Making Moral Decisions

A philosophy instructor at a Massachusetts college had just completed offering a course called Introduction to Ethics. She had given her students a take-home final examination. On the day the exams were due, she collected them from her mailbox and went to her office to read them. She was anxious to see what her students had learned from her course.

After an hour of reading these exams, she was deeply dismayed. Why? Because the more she read, the clearer it became to her that most of her students had cheated.

She called a friend and colleague of hers in the sociology department to share her disappointment not only in her students, but in herself as well. The friend was not surprised. He had just finished reading a report in the *Boston Globe* of a survey that found that 75 percent of all high school students and 50 percent of all college students *admitted* cheating on their exams. A survey conducted by Louis Harris for the Girl Scouts of America found that 65 percent of high school students claimed that they would cheat on a test for which they were not adequately prepared. Another survey revealed the number of confessed cheaters in a variety of professional schools: 63 percent among future lawyers, 66 percent among future public service workers, 68 percent among future physicians, 71 percent among future engineers, and 76 percent among future business managers.

Cheating is a form of stealing, and neither cheating nor stealing is limited to the classroom. For example, the Josephson Institute's "Report Card on American Integrity" found that stealing by teens is increasing. Forty-two percent of teenage boys and 31 percent of teenage girls admitted stealing something at least once a year. Nor is this phenomenon limited to teenagers or college students. For example, the Association of Certified Fraud Examiners reported that about $435 billion is stolen from American businesses each year—by their own workers. This amounts to about 6 percent of the average company's revenues and three times the rate of such fraud estimated in the 1960s. Other recent findings include $100 billion in health care fraud annually, $5 billion in workers' compensation fraud annually, and $100 billion in annual tax cheating. In addition, the *Journal of Business Ethics* found that 47 percent of top executives and 76 percent of graduate-level business students stated that they would commit fraud by understating their firms' write-offs against profits, especially if the chance for job promotion was linked to higher profit figures.

Once I was browsing in a bookstore when I saw a huge volume with an intriguing title: *Wall Street Ethics*. I opened it eagerly, only to find that each of its hundreds of pages was blank.

Opinion poll after poll finds that the problem troubling Americans the most is not national defense or the economy, but the moral condition of society. The apparent unraveling of moral character, especially among our leaders, is a vital concern of most Americans. And well it should be. Without core moral values, the very continuity of a culture is imperiled. As President James Madison warned us, "To suppose that any form of government will secure liberty or happiness without any virtue in the people is a chimerical idea." Indeed, if a foreign power had tried to impose upon us the moral quagmire in which we now seem to find ourselves, Congress might very well have declared a state of national emergency or even war. What is clear, however, is that we are in a state of moral emergency, and we have to do something about it—each of us, and now.

Polls indicate that increasing numbers of people lament the decline in ethical fitness they perceive—from ethnic cleansing in Europe to genocide in Africa, from moral shenanigans in corporate boardrooms to pervasive cheating on tests in the classroom, from abuse in child care centers to corruption in the administration of health care, from duplicity in the White House to moral failing within our own homes.

As our state of moral emergency escalates, as our ethical fitness declines, people seem to want to see ethical behavior—in others, but not necessarily in themselves. They desire integrity in government but continue to vote for and elect politicians who are far from being moral models but who can "get the job done." They want their children to be morally upright, but they fail to admonish them for cheating on exams if it will help them get ahead. They prefer that companies act ethically, but not if it means a decline in jobs and earnings. They condemn organized crime and the criminal acts sometimes committed by sports and media personalities, but they continue to treat such individuals as honored celebrities.

It may be that people do not seek ethical fitness because they have not found a compelling answer to the questions of how and why to be moral, how to be good, and how to make ethical decisions. Ethical fitness begins with responses to these questions.

For a very long time, these questions were answered by referring to certain absolute and universal rules, which were applicable to all times and all places. This was a version of the rule-ethic discussed in chapter 2. Such rules were believed to have been revealed by God, demanded by religious faith, commanded by a monarch, required by the state, imposed by "natural law," or derived from some other source of moral authority. Obedience to these authorities provided an answer to these questions.

One of the features of modern times has been the shift away from accepting an absolute rule-ethic and the authority on which it is based. For example, monarchies are rare today. The state is now understood as a vehicle for reflecting the will of the governed rather than as an instrument for imposing its will on the governed. Many religious people retain faith in God and belief in divine revelation, but they cannot accept as the will of God rules that they find to be either oppressive or irrelevant to the actual conditions in which they find themselves at certain times. Further, as was discussed in the previous chapter, absolute moral rules can become problematic when applied to actual situations. For instance, when telling the truth will place someone's life in danger, it is better to lie. If someone attacks you and tries to kill you, you should defend yourself, even if it means killing your attacker; the rule against not killing has exceptions. Once exceptions are made to the rules, however, the rules themselves become uncertain; the exceptions threaten to become the rules.

As moral absolutism declined and was no longer able to serve as an answer to the question of how to be good, moral relativism came to replace it. Once it became evident that moral relativism could easily slip into ethical anarchy, however, confusion set in. If there are no rules, then perhaps there is no basis for moral behavior, no foundation for ethical decision making.

People tell me that they don't know how to make moral decisions anymore, or even why they should, because "the rules have changed, and I don't know how to behave," because "things aren't as simple as they used to be," or because "things are changing faster than I can."

The rapidly changing conditions that characterize life in our times have made ethical decision making increasingly complex. In recent decades, many of the economic, cultural, and political conditions that we readily assumed to be lasting have been jarred off their moorings. For example, we can no longer depend on a constantly growing economy where children always do better than their parents, a culture where everyone understands and uses the same social rules, or a political climate that rewards true leadership. Many of the values, ideas, and institutions that seemed firmly in place not so long ago have been shaken to their core. Technological developments that populated the realm of science fiction a generation ago are now common fare, bringing with them new problems along with new possibilities. We find ourselves living through an earthquake with its epicenter in the self. Suddenly we realize that the emperor has no clothes, and that the clothes have no emperor. One thing is certain: The future is not what it used to be.

※

It is told that a certain Rabbi Joseph, who lived almost 2,000 years ago, became critically ill and slipped into a coma. His father, Rabbi Joshua, remained by his bedside praying for his recovery. Fortunately, Rabbi Joseph recovered.

When he awoke from his coma, his father asked, "What did you see as you hovered between this world and the next world?"

Said Rabbi Joseph, "I saw a world turned upside down. I saw a topsy-turvy world."

Rabbi Joshua listened, thought for a while, and said, "You saw a clear vision of how things really are. You saw the world clearly."

※

Ours is a topsy-turvy world. From our moorings in the seemingly safe harbor of moral absolutism, we appear to have been cast adrift on the sea of uncertainty of moral relativism, where anything and everything seems to go. While an absolutist ethic can lapse into oppression, paternalism, and inflexibility, a completely relativistic ethic can engender anarchy. When the Bible wants to depict a society as teetering on the brink of moral collapse, it describes such a society as one "where everyone does that which is right in his eyes," that is, where a completely subjective view of ethics leads to chaos. To be sure, if we believe that each person's view is as valid as another's, we might be considered more tolerant than we otherwise might be. But should we allow murder, rape, slavery, torture, and physical abuse, all in the name of tolerance and the exercise of individual moral autonomy?

I find that those who claim that there are no moral values—that ethics is totally relativistic, subjective, and negotiable—usually contradict their expressed views with their own actions. For example, a student in one of my classes wrote a paper trying to defend the view that there is no basis for morality. His paper was well-argued and well-documented. He was proud of his work. He believed that he had proven his case. He had shown his paper to a number of his classmates before submitting it. One of them plagiarized major sections of it and submitted it before he did. When he found out about it, he was overcome with moral outrage. Thus, it seems that people are ready to defend the view that there is no basis for moral actions until someone violates a moral norm and causes them harm.

While understandings of whether certain actions are moral or not may differ from society to society, or even within a society, this does not mean that ethics is completely relativistic. For example, if a person were dropped from a helicopter into any society in the world, and the first thing he did was to murder a respected adult member of that society or take something out of someone's hands and try to run away with it, it is most likely that such an action would be considered by members of that society to be a breach of its moral code. Although societies might express values in different ways, they all hold certain core values in common, such as love, trust, responsibility, and respect for human life. While views of what is a moral action may change from one society to the next, from one age to the next, the conviction that there is such a thing as moral action, that one should be moral, does not change.

The contention that ethics is completely relativistic and subjective is problematic both theoretically and practically. Accepting the notion that there are no core moral values would make it impossible to condemn acts of genocide, torture, and slavery. Rejecting all moral norms would undermine our national affirmation of certain moral values such as liberty, justice, equality, and fairness, and it would stifle our ability to convey these common core values to our children as part of our national heritage. It would remove from our society a foundation for cohesion. It would make a mockery of moral principles taught by religion and would seek to undercut convictions and commitments that provide meaning to people's lives. It would prevent our corporations from articulating a code of ethics, an expression of shared values, that considers some ways of doing business to be appropriate and others not to be.

Codes of ethics need not lead to oppression and to the denial of moral volition. Rather, they may be understood as offering us shared reference points, anchors in a morally complex world. When there is no agreement on core values, then—like in a game with no rules—petty squabbles about every action and movement deflect attention from the larger moral picture.

⊸

Our philosophy professor called a second colleague. This time, it was an instructor in the same department who taught another section of the Introduction to Ethics course. She told her colleague about the exams. He was not surprised.

"On the first day of the course," he said, "I ask my students what kind of behavior they would consider morally wrong. I offer some examples: torturing a child, abusing an invalid in a nursing home, starving someone to death. Here are some of the replies I usually get.

"'Torture and starvation may be bad for you or me, but who are we to say that they are bad for someone else?'

"'When we talk about ethics, whose ethics are we talking about? Yours, mine, our society's? Maybe in certain societies torture, slavery, abuse, and genocide are virtues. Do we have the right to impose our values on others?'

"'Ethics is a matter of personal preference, of taste, like pre-
ferring strawberry ice cream to vanilla. If someone is into torture
and abuse, why not? Whatever turns you on.'

"'If it makes you feel good, it must be good. If it makes you
feel bad, it must be bad. If helping the sick and dying makes you
feel good—go for it. If pulling the wings off butterflies is your
thing, then have a nice day.'"

⊷

As an alternative to absolute ethics, a popular view has
emerged that attempts to ground morality in personal preference.
But can a morality be grounded in individual tastes and fleeting
emotions? Is "I feel like it" or "I like the way it feels" a viable foundation for moral behavior?

How would you react if someone said to you, "I like strawberry ice cream, abusing elderly people, vodka martinis, stealing
clothing from department stores, and a good steak, but I dislike
lime Jell-O, giving charity to help feed hungry children, compassion, and spinach"? You might say that this person has reason-
ably good taste when it comes to food, but bad taste when it
comes to ethics. Or you might say that the preference for certain
foods is a matter of individual taste, while ethical choice is something altogether different, that it is inappropriate to compare
whether or not a person likes vanilla over strawberry ice cream
to whether a person prefers to perform an act of loving-kindness
or to participate in genocide. Yet a popularly pervasive current
view of morality does indeed make these types of comparisons.
Many people believe and act as if moral choice is simply a matter
of personal preference, of individual taste.

Once ethics is reduced to a matter of personal preferences, we
end up with moral anarchy. Every choice—whether it be mercy
or murder—becomes equally valid and beyond dispute. As the famous Latin proverb puts it: *De gustibus non disputandum est.* "In matters of taste, there are no disputes." But taste is not the same as
ought. While it is true that views of what may be morally right or
wrong have changed throughout the centuries, the fundamental
conviction that there *is* right and wrong has not changed.

Another popular view of morality is that it's just a matter of feelings. According to many self-help manuals and pop psychologies, the goal of a full life is to feel good and to be comfortable. But it is only a small jump to equate feeling good with being good, and identifying moral behavior with actions that make a person feel comfortable or good.

According to the "feel good" approach, the basis for determining why and how to be moral is by following one's emotions. Philosophers often call this the emotive theory of ethics. Rather than reviewing the complexities of philosophical argumentation related to this approach, there is a simplified (though not inaccurate) summary of it in an often-quoted remark of Ernest Hemingway: "What I feel good after is probably moral. What I don't feel good after probably is not." Yet feelings are not a reliable barometer for making moral decisions. Feelings are fickle. They change. Love becomes hate, friends become enemies, hopes become disappointments. To be sure, being good and feeling good are not necessarily the same thing. Doing good usually demands discipline, effort, and sometimes sacrifice.

When the propriety of behavior is determined by whether it makes a person feel good about himself—when relationships are forged and maintained on the basis of "whether this is going to work for me now"—temporary feelings, transient needs, and the quest for momentary comfort tend to replace commitment, duty, perseverance, and integrity. Such an approach paradoxically deals with our most intimate and significant experiences within a framework of contractual relations, businesslike trade-offs, and procedural cooperation. Relationships only endure as long as personal needs are met, as long as the relational "contract" is fulfilled. Ironically, in such cost-benefit analysis consensual contracts, obligation and duty become unnecessary, as they are perceived as thwarting the "needs" of the participants. Needs replace commitment. The goal is to feel good rather than to be good. Good and bad actions are replaced by good and bad feelings.

Healing the sick, defending the accused, serving the person in need, creating quality products—all surrender their intrinsic meaning to the quest to feel good. For example, in this view that equates good feelings with good deeds, a rapist who is exhilarated by subjugating and humiliating his victim would have done a morally good thing. On the other hand, a Good Samaritan who helps a person in danger might suffer from injuries and feel bad. He would—in this view that equates how we happen to feel with whether we have acted correctly—have done a bad thing. Such a person would not be a "good" Samaritan.

I often attend meetings where policies are made that affect the lives of others. After a lengthy discussion, someone inevitably asks, "Is everyone comfortable with this?" But what if it were a meeting to determine whether to hire a hit man to kill someone? What if it were a decision to fire all longtime faithful employees? What if everyone present were "comfortable" with such a decision? Should "comfort" be the determining factor of whether one course of action or another is the right thing to do?

Trying to base morality on individual tastes or upon transient feelings is not the only available alternative to an absolutist rule-ethic. For example, for hundreds of years, philosophers and theologians taught that human beings are "rational animals" and that moral behavior means doing what is rational. The rational, they explained, is true, and since the moral is also true, the moral must therefore also be rational. The discoveries of modern psychology, however, have offered a strong refutation to the portrait of the human being as an essentially rational being. Irrationality has been revealed to be as much a part of human nature—or even more of an essential element of human nature—as rationality. Psychologists also have observed that rational behavior often tends to be rationalizing behavior, that is, rational reasons are offered to justify irrational or even horrible behavior. In his autobiography, Bertrand Russell, the Nobel Prize–winning philosopher, said that all his life he believed that Aristotle was right in identifying human beings as rational animals. The only problem, Russell said, is that in all his years, he never met such a human being!

Furthermore, modern philosophers and theologians have shown how a rational morality could be utilized to subvert altruism and love. For example, rationality has been invoked to further the claim that it is not rational, and consequently that it cannot be moral, for a person to set self-interest aside. In this view, altruistic actions, or self-sacrificing actions motivated by love, are dismissed as irrational and hence as amoral or immoral actions. Consequently, the altruistic love of a parent for a child and the self-sacrificing actions of a person such as Mother Teresa would be considered irrational and hence either amoral or immoral. Clearly, the age-old equation of rationality and morality is unable to serve as the primary basis for ethical behavior.

Some people anchor ethics in obedience to social mores. They point out that the etymological root of the word *morality* is "mores," which denotes the customs or usually accepted practices of a particular society or social group. In this view, ethics means following the social norms developed by the society in which we happen to live. Since mores serve as the cement that ensures the cohesion of any particular society, those who are citizens of that society should obey them. A society bereft of norms that govern behavior would readily unravel. What guarantees the continuity of a society is compliance with the shared values that hold it together.

Life is not lived in isolation, but in a society. Consequently, achieving ethical fitness cannot occur in a void. It can only take place within a particular social context. Ethical living relates to a large degree to how we live with others, to how we relate to others. Moral living is predicated upon a declaration of interdependence upon others. For these reasons, norms that flow out of the shared values of a society are crucial in guiding our behavior and in preventing the dissolution of the social or national group to which we belong. Mores offer us a context, a framework, for guiding our behavior, for being good, and for defining how we should live with one another. Social mores teach us what kind of behavior our society considers to be morally good and morally bad. They set down the rules that govern our life in the social context in which our lives are lived out. Without them, social anarchy and moral chaos would likely ensue.

While compliance with social mores is usually *socially* desirable, it is not always *morally* preferable. Social norms can fail to provide a viable foundation for ethical behavior. Just because a certain society considers certain kinds of actions morally good or morally bad does not mean that such actions are actually good or bad. We know of too many examples from all periods of human history of societies that have made rules, established social norms, and taken actions that can hardly be considered moral.

There have been societies in the ancient world that practiced slavery, physical torture, and rape as a matter of social policy. While we may try to excuse them by saying that they were primitive and morally unenlightened societies, we still consider those practices to be morally offensive. Further, what about societies in our own times that practiced and that continue to practice genocide, slavery, torture, and terrorism? Are we willing to accept these practices as morally good because they have been deemed appropriate behavior in a specific society? Were the genocidal policies and practices of Nazi Germany, which had the tacit support of the German people, morally acceptable? Is it justifiable for a society to suppress, imprison, torture, dehumanize, and murder members of minority groups in the name of a higher communal good, or for the protection of the social majority against "infection" allegedly brought about by the very presence of these ethnic minorities? Can the "racial health" of the Aryan race be considered a moral virtue when it leads to the physical extermination of millions of Jews, Slavs, and Gypsies? Was "ethnic cleansing" in Bosnia a social or a moral necessity? Is an action morally right simply because people in a certain society— even the victims—see nothing wrong with it? For example, a female slave in Mauritania was recently asked if she had ever been raped, and if she thought repeated rape was morally wrong. Her reply: "They occasionally come in the night to breed us. Is this wrong? Is this what you mean by rape?"

The view that a society cannot determine what is morally good or bad is not limited to regimes like Nazi Germany or the Stalinist Soviet Union. It also relates to democratic societies. What sometimes eludes us is that neither truth nor morality can really be determined by majority vote or by consensus. What social consensus provides is just that—a consensus, usually reached through a compromise of principles and convictions. A consensus is often a way of trying to make everybody happy while making no one happy.

Public opinion is neither right nor wrong; it is just public opinion. In the movie *Teahouse of the August Moon*, Glenn Ford plays an American officer whose job is to teach democracy to a group of South Pacific Islanders. When they ask him what democracy is, he says, "It's the right of the people to be wrong."

Some years ago, I was asked to evaluate a student teacher who had applied for a teaching license. I entered the classroom and found the students sitting on the floor in a circle around their teacher, stimulated and excited about what she was teaching them. She had transformed a drab classroom into an attractive environment for learning with posters and pictures around the room. One wall contained imaginative drawings done by her first-grade students. My initial impression was very positive. She was, it seemed, a devoted, creative, and effective young teacher. Then came the lesson of the day. The theme was what is democracy.

The class had a pet rabbit who lived in the classroom. The children were being taught responsibility in caring for this rabbit. Now, the rabbit had given birth to a few baby rabbits, and the children enjoyed taking care of the baby rabbits and watching them grow. The teacher gently took one of the baby rabbits from the cage, held it up to the class, and said, "Do any of you know whether this baby rabbit is a boy or a girl?"

The children were embarrassed and began to giggle.

"Now you will learn what democracy is. Democracy means that the majority decides. How many of you think that this is a boy rabbit?"

The boys in the class all raised their hands. One of the girls began to raise her hand, but when she saw that none of the other girls did, she lowered her hand. The teacher counted the raised hands and announced the results.

"There are 12 votes.

"Now, how many of you think that the baby rabbit is a girl rabbit?"

All the girls now raised their hands. The teacher counted the raised hands and said, "There are 14 votes. This means that the majority vote is that the baby rabbit is a girl rabbit. Now let's decide on a girl's name for this little rabbit."

For the next 20 minutes, the students were engaged in an enthusiastic discussion of what to name the baby rabbit, whose sex had been determined by majority vote. Democracy may be the best political system yet devised, but it cannot determine what is either moral or true.

Manners are an example of a social convention that prescribes proper behavior in a particular society. Manners deal with "the right thing to do," but manners and morals are not synonymous. Certain forms of behavior may be considered offensive in polite society in a certain social milieu, but that does not make them immoral. On the other hand, having flawless manners and decorum is no indication of whether a person is moral. Ill-mannered people can be moral, while well-mannered people can be scoundrels.

For example, the biblical prophets, whose teachings serve as the foundation for a great deal of Jewish and Christian morality, were often abrasive, ill-mannered, ill-tempered, and impolite. Yet the morality that they both practiced and taught is a cornerstone of the moral perspective of western civilization. On the other hand, the perpetrators of some of history's most horrendous acts of cruelty, genocide, and torture often possessed impeccable manners and were masters of the social graces. For instance, the infamous Dr. Mengele, who presided over the "selection" process at Auschwitz, was always dressed impeccably, with a starched uniform and white gloves, as he politely separated husbands from wives, parents from children, sending some to slave labor and the others to the gas chambers to be murdered and incinerated.

Strangely, people will readily express discomfort and outrage at a blatant breach of social etiquette that they witness or of which they become aware, but they will remain surprisingly tolerant or apathetic to acts that are morally outrageous. For example, a person slobbering down his soup from a bowl at a dinner party would probably immediately become the object of social ridicule, while whether an act of genocide in a far-off land should be condemned by our government might become an issue for polite, detached, after-dinner conversation.

Neither our personal preferences, nor our emotions, nor the employment of our rational capacities, nor the norms of our society can serve as a reliable foundation for determining why to be moral. Nonetheless, each of these resources can be gainfully employed as tools in helping us make ethical decisions. For example, it would be a waste of our innate and developed talents and abilities not to rationally think through an ethical decision. Nor would it be wise to completely disregard the social norms of our society in trying to determine whether a course of action is morally right or wrong. Neither would it be advisable to ignore our gut feelings, emotions, or intuitions in helping us to come to an ethical decision. Indeed, there are a number of "tests" that may be employed in making ethical decisions that ask us to utilize our emotions, tastes, and intuition.

One is the "yech test." This is your gut-level reaction when you are confronted with an ethical decision. Is one of the options so repulsive that it makes you flinch with physical revulsion? Though you can't clearly articulate why you've reacted the way you have, you are aware that a certain action causes you to recoil. It may well be that this action goes against the grain of your most deeply felt beliefs and values. Indeed, one result of the "yech test" is that it helps to clarify which convictions and values you already embrace. Yet, like all tests, it should be applied with care. People should be careful not to confuse their ethical and their aesthetic responses to the same situation. Recoiling from an offensive odor is not the same as flinching from a distasteful moral option. Indeed, sometimes the most noble moral actions relate to the most unpalatable aesthetic situations. Consider, for example, those people who minister to the poorest of the poor, the sickest of the sick. Their work is not aesthetically pleasing, but it is surely moral.

Another test is the "network nightly news test." How would you react to seeing a story about the action you performed today on tonight's network news, reported all over the country?

Would it be something of which you are proud, or would it be something of which you would be ashamed? If it is something of which you would be ashamed, then it is probably something that is best not to do. Here, too, there is a caveat. You might not want to see something good that you have done on the nightly news simply because you are shy, or humble, or because you fear an invasion of your privacy. Some years ago, the news reported how a miner courageously, and at the risk of his own life, struggled to save a young child trapped in an abandoned mine. The related publicity and probing into every facet of his life led him to regret, on one level, that he had performed this heroic deed.

A third test you might use is the "moral exemplar test." Choose someone you consider to be a moral exemplar, a person you respect as a moral model. Put yourself in that person's place and think about what you are about to do. If you become uneasy, think again. If you do not, that may give you a green light to proceed. For example, in a town in Michigan, people started wearing bracelets with the initials "WWJD," which stood for "What Would Jesus Do?" People there, both adults and children, report that looking at these bracelets often restrains them from doing things they would later regret and encourages them to do virtuous deeds that they otherwise might not do. For instance, one little boy interviewed said that he was about to hit his baby sister, but when he raised his arm to strike her, he saw the letters on his bracelet, and he hugged her instead. Yet, here too, there is a caution: You are not the moral exemplar you are thinking of—you are you. Jesus might have acted in a certain way, but that is a standard toward which many people might aspire but which few, if any, can attain.

Though these three tests are not infallible, and though they're not always decisive in answering the questions of how and why to be moral, they can nonetheless prove helpful in the process of ethical decision making.

✧

A man journeyed through a forest. Enchanted by its beauties, he soon discovered that he was lost. Every path he took to get out of the forest only led him deeper into its labyrinth. After searching for a long time, he saw a man in the distance. Hoping that the man could lead him from the thicket, he ran toward the man.

"Do you know the path out of the confusion of the forest?" he asked the man.

"No," said the man, "for I am also lost in the forest."

Dismayed, the first man began to cry, "How will I ever find my way out of this maze? Will I be lost forever?"

The second man said, "You know paths that do not lead out of the forest. I also know such paths. Perhaps we can share what we know, what we have experienced. And perhaps together, we can find our way out of the forest and into the light."

Why Be Moral?

Your task:
to build a better world, said God.
I answered: How?
The world is such a large, vast place
So complicated now
And I, so small and useless am.
There's nothing I can do.
But God in His great wisdom said:
Just build a better you.

—ANONYMOUS

I see a photograph of a man in a wheelchair, unable to speak or move, afflicted with Lou Gehrig's Disease. I can describe this man by his illness, by what he is no longer able to do. But what does this tell me about him? I might assume that he's helpless, unable to undertake creative endeavors, a person in anguish waiting for an imminent and merciful death. As it happens, though, this man is the great astrophysicist Stephen Hawking, who, though he remains immobile and had his vocal cords surgically removed, continues to communicate his startling theories about the nature of our universe. Further, he is working on ideas that may crack open the very mysteries regarding the existence of everything that is. Show me another person and I can describe him, but does my description capture that individual in terms of his uniqueness, of who he really is?

What do I see when I see another human being? From one

perspective, I see a sample of the species of *Homo sapiens*. I also see, however, a human being unlike any other. We are all born with a unique face; no two faces are identical.

From a scientific perspective, a human being is easily categorized—by species, race, age, sex, height, weight, and so on. The basic statistics on my medical chart, for instance, may be little different from those of thousands of other men. But will a physician reading this chart appreciate who I am? Will he be able to know my cherished hopes and dreams, achievements and aspirations, commitments and loves? Can an examination of the physical functioning of my heart or a scan of my brain discover what feelings populate my heart, what thoughts preoccupy my mind?

Each human being's claim to uniqueness derives not only from who each of us is but even more from who each of us can yet become. Each human soul is like a pod filled with abundant seeds of possibilities waiting to spring forth. Each person has the choice of whether to cultivate or to corrode those seeds. The mission of human existence is for each person to articulate his individual uniqueness by developing the potential that makes him who he is and who he can become. Fulfilling this mission is why each of us is here. It is our life's work.

How each of us develops spiritually and morally, how each of us lives as a human being, expresses how and how well we are fulfilling the mission of human existence. By being good, by cultivating moral virtues like love and empathy, we develop our human potential for goodness. Consequently, one answer to the question of why we should be moral is that being good is indispensable to the fulfillment of our individual mission as a human being.

If we evade our mission, we become like a messenger who has forgotten to deliver the message. Human existence without ethical living is like a premise without a conclusion. Each of us is born a human being. What we can acquire is being human. Being human entails being good.

✧

A friend of mine once was startled after a visit to an art museum.

"What surprised you?" I asked.

"Of all the paintings I saw," he said, "no two paintings were identical. Each was different, unique."

Unlike science, which focuses on universal natural laws, art deals with the unique. The scientist strives to understand what *is* and what *was*, while the artist attempts to create something distinct, unprecedented, new. What makes each of us particularly human is our ability to develop the potential that makes each of us unique. The challenge confronting each person is whether he will allow his life to become a photocopy of many others or to become an original work of art.

A second answer to the question of why we should be moral is that each of us is an artist commissioned to create one great work of art during our own lifetime—and that work of art is our life. Living a moral life is a crucial component in creating one's life as a work of art. The moral virtues, like friendship, loyalty, and humility, are the necessary building blocks for crafting one's life into a work of art.

You are more than flesh, bones, and a bank account. You cannot be defined by a social security number. You are not simply a consumer or a box on an organizational flow chart. You are not an automaton, preprogrammed by genetic, environmental, and social factors. You have aspirations and ambitions, emotions and thoughts. These are revealed in the choices and decisions you make. Through them, you shape your character, your life. Cultivation of the moral virtues such as love, gratitude, and faith provides a vehicle for expressing your character, for responding to the questions of why and how to be moral. Within each human being, there is a work of art waiting to be fashioned. At birth, each of us is issued a passport to transcendence, an invitation to become more than we are. At life's end, I believe each of us will be asked to justify how we have developed the talents and abilities granted us at birth. How will we answer?

The further along we have progressed in crafting life as a work of art, the richer our resources for making ethical decisions.

The more we have developed our humanity, the firmer our foundation for making ethical decisions. Once acquired and refined, the moral virtues fashion our character and provide a basis for moral living, for being good. For example, if you develop the virtue of love, you will be loving. If you develop the virtue of friendship, you will be a good friend to have. The beliefs, convictions, and values that you cherish constitute the ingredients and the tools you already possess that can be utilized in making particular ethical decisions. How well you have developed these components of creating life as an art form will shape the nature and the quality of the decisions you make.

An athlete does not enter a championship play-off without considerable prior training. If called upon to participate, he wants to be in the best shape possible. Similarly, the moral life, or being good, demands our continuous attention. Cultivation of the moral virtues molds who we are, who we can yet become, and the ethical choices that we are called upon to make. It helps assure that we are ethically fit, morally able to deal with the ongoing challenges posed by daily living, and ethically prepared to confront the occasional moral crises that punctuate our lives, usually with little advance warning.

Focusing upon the cultivation of virtue offers a viable alternative to the rigidity of moral absolutism and the anarchy of moral relativism. Virtues are not absolutes; they are guides that point a way toward the spiritual augmentation of the self. In creating one's life as a work of art, the moral virtues, such as sincerity, integrity, and humility, serve as directional signals. Rather than providing a long list of shoulds and shouldn'ts, they offer a map that enables each person to become more fully human. Each of us is given a choice: to let the soul atrophy or to allow it to flourish. We are born as originals. We can die either as copies or as developed, original works of art.

⚭

Which ingredients are required to produce a great work of art? Which ingredients are needed to create one's life as a work of art?

The first ingredient in creating life as a work of art is maturity, which means taking responsibility for your own life and your own decisions. We do not expect moral behavior from a baby because it is not yet mature. Maturity is seen in the values that a person has and how these values are applied to situations that he encounters. Moral maturity is the message of the biblical story of Adam and Eve in the Garden of Eden.

God commanded Adam and Eve not to eat of the forbidden fruit in the Garden. But they ate anyway. What was their sin? Most biblical commentators say it was disobedience to God's command not to eat the forbidden fruit. However, another interpretation is possible. When God asked Eve if she ate the forbidden fruit, Eve answered that the serpent made her do it. When God asked Adam, Adam answered that Eve made him do it. This means that the real sin was not disobeying God, but that it was blaming someone else for their mistakes instead of taking responsibility for their deeds. What Adam and Eve told God was that they should not be held responsible for what they did because someone else made the decision for them, that someone else should be responsible. In summary, Adam and Eve showed a lack of maturity.

Johnny, who was four, shared a room with his baby brother. One day, Johnny was playing in his room when he decided that the rug in his room should be another color. Though he knew it was wrong, he used his Magic Marker to begin the task of changing the color of the rug. His mother came into the room and was horrified. Johnny got frightened, and he pointed to his infant brother, sleeping blissfully in the nearby crib, and said, "He made me do it."

A major obstacle that stifles our ability to create our lives as works of art is the belief that we are bereft of choice and responsibility. Ethical living, being good, entails the ability to actively and deliberately craft our lives as works of art. The other choice is to remain life's victim, avoiding responsibility, blaming others for all of our problems, and wallowing in our misfortunes—real and imagined. Crafting life as a work of art entails moral maturity, which requires making deliberate choices and taking responsibility for them.

If a person's moral choices are predetermined, if an individual is simply a puppet controlled by external forces, then making moral choices becomes meaningless. Only with choice can there be responsibility and spiritual and moral self-development. According to the Talmud, even God does not interfere with our ability to make moral choices. God creates each of us as a free moral agent. God desires each of us to become morally mature, to create our lives as works of art.

A Talmudic legend tells that when a child is conceived, Leila, the angel of the night, brings the fetus before God. The angel asks, "Will this child be tall or short?" and God decrees its height.

"Will this child be smart or not smart?" and God decrees its intellectual capacity.

Then the angel asks, "Will this child be good or bad?" and God is silent—because moral volition is not a matter of divine decree, not a matter of predestination, but of individual choice.

In a real way, a human being is the sum of choices he makes over a lifetime. We inevitably reach a point when it is time to choose, to act—even if it ends up as not being the best or the right choice. Not making any choice leads us to anxiety, to helplessness, to spiritual and moral paralysis. In this regard, consider the old story of Buridan's donkey.

The medieval philosopher Buridan had a donkey who, like its master, was a philosopher. One day, rather than offering the donkey his morning bale of hay, Buridan offered the donkey two equal bales of hay. The donkey spent the entire day trying to decide which bale of hay to eat. But the donkey could not decide which bale of hay was the better one. This went on day after day—until the donkey, unable to decide, starved to death.

In a way, human existence is a game of "You Bet Your Life." We must take the risk of making a choice, even though it might be the wrong choice. Each of us must take a leap of commitment before we starve to death viewing the repast of options set out before us.

We are presented with a range of choices not only in ethical situations but also in almost every aspect of our daily lives. For example, not so long ago, ordering a cup of coffee in a restaurant was a simple and straightforward matter. Now, there are choices: regular, decaf, espresso, café au lait, and so on. Once the kind of coffee has been decided, there are choices of sweeteners, such as sugar, artificial sweetener, cinnamon, raw sugar, and brown sugar. Then comes the question of whether to have cream, milk (regular, 2 percent, 1 percent, or skim), nondairy creamer, and so on. Simply ordering a cup of coffee has become like a multiple-choice exam. Or go for some ice cream. Not so long ago, there were the standard flavors: vanilla, chocolate, strawberry. Now, one has to choose from myriad flavors, not to mention varieties such as low-fat, sugar-free, and nondairy.

The French philosopher Jean-Paul Sartre was correct when he characterized life in our times as being "condemned to freedom." We are constantly being bombarded by choices. While making ethical decisions always has been complex, it is perhaps more complicated today because of the increasing number of choices we are called upon to make and because of the escalating number of options to be weighed and considered when making each choice. But the ethical choices we make do not emerge out of a void. They are not made from scratch. They are grounded in convictions that we already affirm, in moral values that we already embrace, in relationships that we value, in what matters to us most.

The second ingredient in creating one's life as a work of art is the study of past masterpieces. An apprentice artist must study the works and techniques of the great masters before trying to compose a great work of his own. Similarly, we turn to the spiritual maestros of the past to study the techniques they developed in the art of living. We stand in awe of the masterpieces that are each of their lives. Each aspiring artist studies the works of those great artists who came before.

We would never buy a house or a car or deal with matters of our health without expert advice or without consulting those with knowledge and experience. Yet we take our most valuable possession, our life, and allow it to develop without consultation with the wisdom of the past. To disregard the spiritual resources we have inherited from the past is to squander a much-needed and readily accessible heritage. To relinquish hard-won cumulative wisdom and experience and to expect to develop our souls on our own is misguided conceit. We seem to forget that extraordinarily wise people have preceded us, and that they have grappled with many of the problems that perplex us today. Being good can be facilitated by tapping into the substantial resources bequeathed to us by past tradition and experience. It only makes sense that we ought to consult present and past wisdom figures. These physicians of the human soul can serve as our teachers in the art of soul-crafting.

It is our spiritual dimension that ensures our uniqueness and that makes each of us who we are and who we can yet become. There has never been another human being like you, like your beloved, or like your child. You may believe that uniqueness is limited to your fingerprints or to your DNA, but if you believe that there is more, that there is an ineffable, sublime essence to being human, then how will you honor it? How will you nurture and develop it? Souls can grow. The aim of life is to end it with a soul more beautiful than when we began. Ethical living, cultivation of the moral virtues, is a way of nurturing our spiritual development. It is an essential pathway to the creation of life as a work of art. The wisdom offered by past cartographers of the human soul offers us maps for the creation of life as the highest art form.

A third ingredient is the cultivation of wisdom, the ability to understand what we know, to evaluate what we have experienced and learned. Knowledge is critical, but it's not sufficient. Knowledge of the insights bequeathed to us from the past is enriching, but it is of little value unless we have the wisdom to employ it.

Scripture tells us, "Wisdom is the principal thing; therefore, get wisdom" (Proverbs 4:7). Yet Scripture also reminds us that wisdom is rare, elusive, and therefore precious: "Wisdom, where shall it be found . . . it cannot be gotten for gold?" (Job 28:12, 15).

But what is the nature of wisdom? What characterizes this price-less commodity?

It would be a mistake to identify knowledge with wisdom, perception with insight, or erudition with understanding. Knowl-edge is a readily accessible commodity. The computer age liter-ally has placed infinite quantities of information, knowledge, and data at our fingertips. Knowledge can be "accessed" and "processed," but wisdom cannot. While the sciences have much to say about knowledge, they have almost nothing to say about wisdom.

There is no wisdom at first sight. It is an acquisition that must be pursued as well as a gift that must be bestowed. As the Talmud states, "One who has acquired wisdom has acquired everything. One who has acquired wisdom, what does he lack? One who lacks wisdom, what has he acquired?"

Wisdom entails discernment—the ability to make perceptive judgments rather than only expedient decisions. It asks us to ques-tion answers as well as to answer questions and to anticipate long-range consequences rather than to be satisfied with meeting only short-term needs. Wisdom counsels us against confusing mo-mentary whims with lifelong aspirations, transient pleasures with spiritual fulfillment, and the satisfaction of our needs with au-thentic happiness. Without wisdom, advantages like health, wealth, success, power, honor, and prestige are ultimately useless because without wisdom, a person will not know how to benefit from them.

According to St. Thomas Aquinas, a characteristic of wisdom is "the ability of seeing through things." The wise person tries to pierce the veil of appearances that restricts our clear vision of our-selves and of our world. He is not duped into self-deception by his own vanity. The value of wisdom is that it points to what mat-ters most, to what is valuable.

Wisdom is the bridge between knowledge and action, be-tween belief and virtue. A wise decision is a good decision. As Plato said, "There can be no virtue without wisdom." Without wisdom, the soul is blind, but without correlative deeds of virtue, life becomes lame. Virtue and wisdom are the twin sisters of the moral life, of being good. The moral virtues are the engine, and wisdom is the rudder that drives life in the direction of being good, that propels us in the creation of life as an art form. Virtue is the disposition of acting in accordance with wisdom. A person's character is the sum total of developed virtues.

A fourth ingredient is imagination. We need to transcend ourselves in order to envision who we yet can become. Without imagination, without vision, an artist has nothing to express, nothing to convey. Neither the life of art nor the art of life can move to a higher plane without dreams.

In one episode of *Star Trek: The Next Generation*, a strange malady inexplicably affects the members of the crew. People become anxious and irritable. Some go insane. Then they start to die. Tests are run, but the cause of the strange illness cannot be identified by any means of medical diagnostic technology. In discussing the situation, the crew members discover that they have something in common, something that they initially had overlooked, something that might be the cause of the affliction. What they find out is that for some reason, the crew members had stopped dreaming. A drug is prepared that reintroduces dreams into the sleep cycle. As a result, people begin to dream again. The crisis passes. The same lesson is taught by the biblical prophets: "Without vision the people perish." To live our dreams and to reach our goals, however, disciplined use of our abilities and skills is required.

A fifth ingredient is careful use of our already developed skills in achieving our goals. One wrong stroke of an artist's brush can ruin a painting. One wrong note can ruin a symphony. One wrong act can mar a life. A Hasidic master once said that we should consider ourselves tightrope walkers, wearing white garments, with bottles of ink on our heads. One small wrong step and the ink soils the garment. One big wrong step and we fall into the abyss below. Great art is not the product of fleeting inspiration. Rather, it requires careful and constant exertion. As Thomas Edison put it, "Genius is 1 percent inspiration, 99 percent perspiration."

On one side of the spectrum, there are those people who misuse their skills because their goals exceed their abilities. To strive to achieve the unreachable goal only invites frustration and despair. On the other side of the spectrum, however, there are those people who sell themselves short. These include human beings who seek the security of inaction by underestimating their skills and abilities, who feign humility to avoid responsibility, and who are eminently able but who pretend to be disabled when a difficult but achievable challenge is brought before them. They then wonder why they feel disillusioned, unfulfilled, anxious, and despondent. Yet, in the deepest recesses of their souls, these people know that, as Pogo puts it, "We have met the enemy, and they are us." They are somehow aware that as their life's motto, they have chosen a revised version of the old adage "There but for me, goes I."

Challenges and goals require appropriate skills. When challenges are high and correlative skills and abilities are low, an activity becomes meaningless and evokes anxiety. When challenges are low and skills and abilities are high, a feeling of boredom and listlessness emerges. When challenges are high and skills and abilities are up to the purpose at hand and are utilized to the utmost, however, a person can experience a rare sense of heightened consciousness, an enviable sense of accomplishment, and a desirable state of self-fulfillment. Such a state has been called flow by psychologist Mihaly Csikszentmihalyi, professor at the University of Chicago and author of numerous books. Others have described it as a state of life satisfaction. It is very similar to the transcendence or ecstasy that is described in a wide variety of mystical traditions. For people who are engaged in crafting their lives as works of art, the challenge is to be who we are by using our talents and our skills in order to become more than we ever expected to be. In this way, we can achieve more than we ever thought possible.

↔

When the great Hasidic master Zusya of Anipol was on his deathbed, he began to cry. His disciples asked, "Master, why do you cry? Do you cry because you are afraid that when you arrive before the Heavenly Tribunal, they will ask, 'Why were you not like Isaiah, or like Maimonides?'"

"No," said Zusya. "I am not worried that they will ask me that because I was not a prophet like Isaiah nor a great philosopher like Maimonides. I am neither a prophet nor a philosopher."

"Then why are you crying, master?" his disciples asked Zusya once again.

"Because," he said, "I am afraid they will ask me, 'Zusya, why weren't you like Zusya? Why weren't you yourself? Why weren't you all that you could be?' If they ask me that, what shall I answer?"

⊶ 5 ⊷

The Communion of Love

Put love first.

—I CORINTHIANS 14:1

*T*here he was with big blue eyes, hungry and naked, looking as amazed to see me as I was to see him: my son. It was love at first sight—or even before. He was a mess, and he was tired after his journey from the womb to the world. It had been a long day. I looked lovingly at my wife who was simultaneously exhilarated and exhausted. We celebrated the co-creation of our procreation. We both knew that our lives would never be the same again, and we both relished the thought.

A few days later, he and my wife came home from the hospital. Late that night, with my wife fast asleep, I awoke and heard him crying. Stricken with the panic of a new father, I ran into his room. Why was he crying? Was he sick or hurt? No—only wet. I cleaned him off and changed his diaper, a process which unexpectedly gave me great joy. I took him into the guest room, lay down on the bed, and placed him stomach down on my stomach. We were alone at last. I looked at him and said, "I'm very happy you are here." He looked up at me and smiled—maybe it was gas, maybe not. I stared at him until he fell asleep. Soon, I was asleep as well. As I think back on all the many moments that have been my life, that moment when he smiled—gas or not—was the happiest moment of my life.

Everything he did became an event of metaphysical significance, whether it was a bowel movement or a leg movement. Each was a marvel. I would watch him for hours and think to myself, "Surely, in human history, there has never been a child like this!"

There he was, helpless in his crib, needing our aid to meet his most fundamental needs, simply to live. Yet his very existence fulfilled my deepest needs: the need for meaning, the need to express love, the need to be needed. As the Talmud puts it, "More than the calf needs to suck, does the cow need to suckle."

Today we tend to equate erotic love with sexual attraction, but for the ancient Greeks, "eros" referred to an attraction that was hoped would complete and fulfill the person. In this view, the truly erotic relationship is one that makes us more than we are, that promises to transform us to be the best we can become. It is characterized by interdependence. Indeed, love is a declaration of interdependence.

It is popular today to focus discussions of love upon conjugal love. But love comes in many forms of which conjugal love is but one. We tend to think that sex will lead us to a better understanding of love. In fact, the opposite is often true: Love can lead us to a better understanding of sex. Mastering sexual techniques will not necessarily amplify our ability to love, but cultivating the ingredients that constitute love promises to enhance the quality of our sexual experience. There are forms of love where love and sex coalesce in passionate pandemonium. And there are forms of love that require passion though not sexuality. These include the love of a parent for a child, the love of work, the love for God, the love for a friend, and the love of country.

For the person who loves, life is never devoid of meaning. Other moral values may contribute to a life of meaning—like faith, integrity, or courage—but love does more than contribute to meaning; love underlies it. For a person without love, life is an empty shell, a hollow vessel, a lonely journey.

I have never met a person who could say without the most profound regret, "I cannot love." Nothing dramatizes the centrality of love to life more than the absence of love in life. St. Paul understood this well when he said, "I may . . . know every hidden truth; I may have faith strong enough to move mountains, but if I have not love, I am nothing. . . . There are three things that last forever: faith, hope, and love; but the greatest of them all is love" (1 Corinthians 13).

True love must not only be love but also it must be true. To be true, it must not be counterfeit. It must not be something else pretending to be love. What passes for love is often a case of mistaken identity. How can we tell the difference between counterfeit love and true love?

One vital sign is the test of singularity. Suppose someone whom you think you love is lost to you forever—either through death or another type of permanent separation. You are then offered an exact double of that person—with the same looks, the identical gestures, the same voice. Would this, or any replacement, be satisfactory? If the answer is no, then you are probably in love. That we can continue to love someone, to feel their presence, and to be influenced by them even after their death demonstrates that love primarily relates to the distinctive essence of an individual rather than to their physical presence. A lost beloved is irreplaceable precisely because he is unique. Replaceability is not a feature of true love.

Friends of mine, Joel and Eleanor, lost their daughter Jackie to leukemia. Jackie was nine years old when she died. Their grief was understandably inconsolable. Our mutual friend Blanche paid a condolence call. Trying to ease their grief, she said, "Don't worry. You're both young. You can still have a child to replace Jackie." Blanche meant well, but she failed to understand that a beloved is irreplaceable, unique. The litanies of love celebrate uniqueness: There's just no one like her; When they made him, they threw away the mold; You're one of a kind; I've never met anyone like you before. It is not the idea of love that I love, but particular individuals. The view that love must include or lead to the love of all people is a fallacy. If I love everyone, then I love no one. If everyone is "special," then no one is "special." If I love all children equally, then in what way is my love for my own child particular and unique?

If I want my child to be what I could not be, if I want him to be a fulfillment of my fantasies rather than his own, then I do not accept him in his uniqueness. I love not him—but rather, like Narcissus, I have fallen in love with the reflection of an image of myself. Love means recognizing, celebrating, and encouraging the unfolding of the individuality of another. Love means acceptance of whom the other person is and can become, instead of considering him a servant of our needs, a projection of our desires, or an object of our dependencies. In love, not my needs but the needs of the person I love become paramount. Love entails a level of intimacy where we know the needs and desires of someone other than ourselves.

In the masquerade ball where a variety of pretenders come attired as love, we can unmask infatuation pretending to be love. While love recognizes the unique singularity of the beloved, infatuation focuses instead upon the "significant other" as the fulfillment of a type, a category, or a fantasy being sought. Infatuations objectify the other person in terms of something they have (for example, a great body, fame, fortune, or social status) rather than in terms of who they really are. Infatuation is the twin of narcissism because it is rooted in our own desires, needs, and insecurities, rather than in the acceptance of the uniqueness of the other. There is an old Yiddish proverb that catches the tenor of mutual infatuation: They're madly in love—he with himself, she with herself.

⌇

Late one night, the phone rang. It was my friend Alex. Since his divorce, he had immersed himself in the exhilarations and disappointments of the singles scene. I had not heard much from him for some months.

"I've found her," Alex said, even before telling me it was him.

"Who?" I asked.

"Her," he said, "the woman of my fantasies."

"Tell me about her."

"She has a great body . . . (which he then described in the most intimate detail), a great job, a trust fund, and her uncle was the state attorney general. She's good for me and good for business."

"Alex," I interrupted. "By the way, what's her name?"

"Oh, yeah," he said. "It's Jill."

"Does she want to have children? How does she get along with your kids? What are her deepest fears? What is her favorite flower, her favorite flavor of ice cream?"

"I don't have a clue," Alex said. "We spend too much time together in bed to talk much."

⌒

Alex was infatuated by Jill, but not in love with her. Sometimes infatuation can move to a higher level of love; often it does not. In his classic work *The Art of Loving*, psychoanalyst Erich Fromm described these two levels in this way, "Immature love says: I love you because I need you. Mature love says: I need you because I love you."

In biblical Hebrew, *yada* means both to love and to know. Without knowledge of the other, love is a fleeting emotion, a sentiment without depth. Knowledge requires communication. Communication is vital because it is the prelude to self-disclosure and intimacy. Revealing our innermost core to another and receiving the disclosure of the other is how knowledge becomes part of a loving relationship. In the mirror of the eyes of our beloved, we see ourselves as we really are, without deceptions and without masks. Through the window of the eyes of our beloved, we embrace the soul of another self in all of its uniqueness. Love is disclosure; it is revealing. But disclosure is a risk that presumes trust. Only with trust can we share convictions, hopes, joys, fears, and dreams.

Intimate communication has become increasingly rare in our era of sophisticated public relations and crippled private relations, our times of high tech but low touch. Many people find themselves "intimacy challenged," unable to communicate with others. Many are like the man who resigned from his fear of intimacy support group because he was afraid that the other people there were getting too close. It seems that the more advanced our technology of communication becomes, the less developed the art of interpersonal communication becomes.

⊸

The lights were dimmed, and violins played romantic music in the gourmet restaurant. I was dining with guests from Europe who were in the process of overcoming their skepticism about the possibility of finding "high cuisine" in a middle-American city. At a table nearby, two lovers met. It was obviously the beginning of what was supposed to be an evening of intense romance and passion. They looked at one another with adoring eyes. On the table, their extended hands touched one another at the fingertips, and under the table, their feet found one another as preludes of the physical intimacy that would ensue later that evening. Suddenly, the man reached for his hip, extracted a beeper from his belt, read an encrypted message, took out a tiny phone from his pocket, withdrew his hand from hers, and began to speak in an animated way with someone, somewhere, whom she could neither see nor hear. After a few minutes, she removed a cellular phone from her purse and began to speak with deep attention to someone somewhere else. Their respective conversations continued as various courses were served. The bill came. Each completed their calls. He paid the bill. They left, though not hand in hand.

⊸

A "relationship" is not love. Like a well-oiled machine, a relationship can function well for many years while the parties involved remain cohabiting strangers. Love with the perfect stranger is not true love. Only through the intimacy and trust of knowledge and disclosure can love ensue.

My friend Mitchell's wife died of the quick ravages of pancreatic cancer, leaving him a widower in his early forties with four young children. One day he found a diary his wife had kept since they were married. He read it and realized that all those years he had lived with a stranger. Her reactions to experiences that they had shared caught him completely by surprise. "The person she describes in the diaries as me was a stranger to her and to me as well," he tearfully told me. What Mitchell told me reminded me of what philosopher Sam Keen describes as destructive fidelity, by which he means a love relationship that has disintegrated into a "shared addiction"—a bad habit that no one has the power to break.

Through intimate knowledge of another, three new beings are created. Love changes me, extending and deepening the contours, the identity of my innermost self. I become a new person because of intimacy with my beloved. If my beloved reciprocates, my beloved also becomes someone new, someone renewed. And, in the matrix of love where the boundaries between ourselves and the person we love become fuzzy, a third new being is created, a being called "we." In love, we move from me to we. In love, $1+1=1$.

⌒

A couple about to be married came to see me to talk about the service that I had agreed to perform. They had an unusual request. They each wanted to say the following to one another at the service: "I will honor and love you—as long as things continue to work out." I refused under these circumstances to perform the wedding.

⌒

Locked within the fortress of the ego, we watch for and critique the flaws of others, convincing ourselves that prudence demands caution in committing ourselves to another, to accepting someone as that person is. We may be ready to offer a contract—but only if our conditions are met. Love, however, is not a contractual matter of give and get. It is not a listing on any commodities exchange. To the contrary, love is rooted not in appraisal but in bestowal. There is a value in the beloved that is beyond evaluation.

Love is not a "limited partnership" with tentative commitments. It is an unconditional commitment without warranties. Contractual love cannot be mutually satisfying over the long haul. An accounting ledger recording credits and debits is not the hallmark of a love relationship. To determine if a contract works, one has to evaluate it objectively and coldly. Nothing cools off the heat of passionate love as much as a cost-benefit analysis. Devotion differs from a conditional agreement.

Love is born in wonder. It is bestowed because of astonishment, not accomplishment. It is offered simply because someone is loved. I love my son because I am amazed at the sheer marvel of his existence. He need not earn my love. My love is not an award that he must win by means of successful competition.

⊷

I go to my son's Little League game. The game drags on. I am thinking about other things I could be doing. But now my son comes to the plate. My thoughts shift. My attention focuses on him. Whether or not he gets a hit may not decide the game, yet my heart begins to race. I can stand up before a thousand people and deliver a controversial speech without having an anxiety attack. I can offer media-byte comments to the press without a twinge. I can engage in complex negotiations without skipping a beat. But my son is at the plate, and I am a nervous wreck. Why am I in such a state? I care because he cares. I care because the outcome of his swing will bring him either joy or dismay. If he gets a hit, I will share his excitement; if he does not, I will feel his disappointment. Empathy is an ingredient of love. Love is never a spectator sport.

The opposite of empathy and love is not hate, but apathy. Love that turns to hate can turn back to love, but love that dissipates into apathy can't readily be reclaimed. It was the infamous Marquis de Sade who advocated and admired the cultivation of *apetie*, apathy, and who disparaged empathy and love. Once a person becomes care-less, the soul atrophies and begins to wither. Apathy is not only a retreat from passion but also a retreat from the virtues of courage and commitment that love demands. Since love requires giving without the guarantee of receiving, intimacy along with the exposure of vulnerability, love demands courage— taking a risk, even though it might lead to pain and disappointment.

Empathy means seeing and being in a situation as another sees it and feels it. It means sharing joy as well as pain, exaltation as well as disappointment. It means trying to practice the biblical injunction to love another as you love yourself.

Self-love is both a danger and an opportunity. It can serve as a vehicle either to self-absorption or to self-awareness, to obsession with the self or to empathy with another. Loving others and love of the self exist in a feedback loop. Loving another can provide a reason to love ourselves; self-love can extend our capacity to love beyond ourselves. Paradoxically, through loving another, our own esteem, worth, and validation become amplified. Being in love with someone other than ourselves can spur us on to take better care of our own selves than we might otherwise. Suddenly, there is an impetus beyond our own selves that is gently pushing us to tend to our health, to mend our harmful habits, to develop our innate abilities.

Empathy entails care, which is a crucial ingredient in the recipe for love. Without care, love is reduced to trivial sentimentality, a passing fancy, or an episode of transitory passion. Care is a skill to be cultivated. It demands constant attention, concern, and commitment. There is an old saying: "Love is like bread. It has to be made fresh daily." To love means to care, even if it breaks our heart. As Rabbi Nahman of Bratzlav said, "There is nothing as whole as a broken heart."

Love that remains sentiment cannot endure. Love must also be commitment articulated in concrete deeds. In this regard, consider a note a teenage boy once sent his girlfriend.

Dearest Jane,

My love for you is higher than the highest mountain, deeper than the deepest sea. My heart skips a beat each time I think of you. I cannot live without you. I ache every moment to see you.

Love,
John

P.S. If it is raining Saturday night, I can't take you out because I don't want to catch a cold.

While John professes a deep love for Jane, he's not willing to inconvenience himself for her. His love is in writing only. In any case, what John also doesn't realize is that there is truth in the old adage, "If you don't want to catch a cold, fall in love." Studies have shown that exposure to love heightens the immune system. For example, a group of Harvard students were shown a documentary of Mother Teresa lovingly ministering to the sick. After the film, they had their saliva tested. They were found to have elevated levels of certain antibodies, including those that prevent colds and other infections. Further, a study of 10,000 men with heart disease found a 50 percent reduction in the frequency of chest pain (angina) in men who perceived their wives as supportive and loving.

In the fifteenth century, the alchemist Paracelsus wrote that "the main reason for healing is love." More recently, physician Larry Dossey has written, "If scientists suddenly discovered a drug that was as powerful as love in creating health, it would be heralded as a medical breakthrough and marketed overnight—especially if it had as few side effects and was as inexpensive as love. Love is intimately related with health. This is not a sentimental exaggeration."

Love is an art, and like the art of life, the art of love must be developed, cultivated, and maintained. Love is a virtue, and it is intertwined with other virtues such as empathy, humility, compassion, wisdom, courage, trust, gratitude, and loyalty. No matter when, between whom, or how many times it happens, love is always for the first time—always new, renewing, and invigorating. Each meeting is a new adventure, generating meaning, enchantment, beauty, and hope.

The moral values are the building blocks for creating life as a work of art. Love is the queen of the virtues, however, because it reveals to us those relationships, convictions, and commitments that we value most highly. Love indicates what matters most to us, what we find most meaningful.

And so it happened that the beautiful maiden named Psyche fell in love with and was loved by Eros, the god of love. Each night Eros would visit his beloved Psyche, but only on the condition that she would never ask his name or look upon his face. But one night while Eros slept, Psyche awoke, lit a lamp, and looked upon her beloved Eros resting in a blissful sleep. Eros awoke from his slumber, and he knew that Psyche had looked upon his face. Out of anger, Eros fled, leaving Psyche at the mercy of his mother, the goddess Aphrodite. Yet Psyche would surrender neither her beloved nor her love. She defied gods and goddesses and wandered in search of her lover. After an arduous and relentless search, Psyche found Eros and was reunited with him. For her persistent love, Psyche was granted immortality. Ever since then, Psyche has symbolized the human soul, because the vocation of the soul is to seek out and to find love.

6

The Attitude of Gratitude

*If you cannot be grateful for what you have received, then
be thankful for what you have been spared.*

—YIDDISH PROVERB

s in most American cities, in downtown Chicago
where I work, one encounters homeless people.
They stand on the streets, begging for money and for
food. Some hold up signs asking for help. Mostly, people just ignore them and pass them by. Yet there is one homeless man who
stands in front of an office building in downtown Chicago who
people rarely pass by. They inevitably reach into their pockets and
hand him some money, no matter how rushed they seem. They
smile at him both with sadness and encouragement, and then they
go on their way. One day, I watched for a while, trying to figure
out why he of all the homeless people evokes such an unusual response. Then I went closer to him and saw the sign he carries. I
understood. His sign reads, "I was once like you, but one day you
might be like me. So help me, please."

Seeing that reminded me of a story I once read about the
great German writer Goethe during his celebrated Italian
journey. Goethe was visiting St. Peter's Cathedral. He saw many

71

blind beggars crouching at their posts near the entrance to the church, displaying crudely written appeals for coins. Goethe grew increasingly intrigued as he noticed the worshipers and visitors passing by most of the beggars. Almost invariably, they paused to drop a coin into a cup held out by one of them—always the same one. Often, a stroller who thoughtlessly passed by would turn around, come back to this specially favored blind beggar, donate something, and resume his promenade. Filled with curiosity, Goethe thrust himself into the procession of visitors and read as he moved along, again and again, in one style or another, "Help the blind." Finally, he reached the station of the beggar whose sign seemed to work such wonders. It said, "It is springtime. The flowers and the trees are in bloom. But I am blind."

Do we have to lose our sight to be grateful for the gift of sight? Do we have to suffer a loss before we can appreciate what and who are most precious to us? Not taking for granted the many gifts and bounties that populate our daily lives with blessings is a crucial component in instilling the attitude of gratitude.

Each day, we hear and read of calamities that unexpectedly afflict other people: the death of a loved one, the diagnosis of a terminal or debilitating disease, the loss of a job, the failure of a relationship, an accident, a natural catastrophe. The pages of our newspapers and the news stories on our airwaves are saturated with reports of human tragedies. If we look carefully at what surrounds us, we are drawn to realize that there is so much from which we have been spared and, consequently, so much for which we have to be grateful.

Ask most parents what would be the worst calamity they could imagine happening to them, and they will tell you it is the loss of a child. Parents who have suffered the inconsolable loss of a child as well as couples trying to overcome infertility to have a child realize only too well what parents sometimes forget—the immeasurable preciousness of a child, the inexpressible meaning and joy that a child's very existence brings to those who love that child. In the midst of the hectic lives we live, the nagging demands that children often place upon us sometimes lead us to forget how empty our lives would be without them.

⊷

In an affluent suburban community on Chicago's North Shore, a deranged man walked into an elementary school one day and shot randomly at a class of fourth-graders. Three died. Others were wounded. I knew one of the parents of one of the children in that school. "I hug my kid a lot more than I used to," this austere business executive confessed to me. "I never before realized how much I love my daughter, how very much it means to me to see her home safe every evening, and how grateful I am that her life is part of my own life. Unfortunately, it took this tragedy for me to realize what I already should have known."

⊷

Meeting a person who cannot see can evoke our gratitude for the gift of sight that we so readily take for granted. Losing our breath, even for a moment, can lead us to appreciate and to be grateful for the gift of breath, which is the gift of life. Seeing a person confined to a wheelchair can remind us that simply being able to walk, or to walk without pain, is something not to be taken for granted. Until confined, we often fail to appreciate the gifts of freedom and mobility. When we are deprived of food and drink, even for a day, we are inevitably drawn to appreciate the delights of food and drink. When a prisoner of war who had been held in Vietnam for many years finally returned home, what he wanted to do first was to have a hamburger. For him, eating that hamburger signified an end to hunger, deprivation, and captivity. Seeing those who live in abject poverty can evoke our gratitude not only for the conveniences that we have but also for the necessities of life that we tend to regard as entitlements. Being aware of those who live under oppressive political regimes can make us increasingly appreciative of the fundamental liberties and rights that we enjoy in a free society.

Ideally, it should not take a loss, or the contemplation of a loss, of what we have to evoke in us the attitude of gratitude. Realizing the many calamities from which we have been spared is not the best way to cajole us into appreciating the blessings that we enjoy. Yet many people remain oblivious to the gifts that are theirs until faced with the possibility of losing them.

There are a number of levels that characterize the attitude of gratitude. The lowest is failing to appreciate the preciousness of what we have until we are confronted with the loss of it. A higher level is being grateful for what we now have but did not always have. Often those who were once denied something tend to appreciate it once they have it, more so than those who always have had it. Let me offer one example.

I was wheeling my shopping cart down the aisle at the local supermarket when I noticed the supermarket manager and two policemen detaining a Black man. I asked one of the clerks what the problem was, and she told me that this man often came to the supermarket, that he would wander around for hours without a shopping cart or a shopping basket, and that he rarely bought anything. He was being held for loitering and for suspicion of robbery. I wheeled my cart closer to where the man was being questioned, and to my surprise, he motioned to me to come over to talk to the police on his behalf. As I approached, I recognized him. He had been a student of mine some years before. In fact, he was an Ethiopian Jew. I introduced myself to the policemen and to the manager and asked what the problem was. They confirmed what the clerk already had told me. So I asked him, "Why are you wandering around this supermarket?" He said, "I wander around many supermarkets, department stores, and drug stores, too." The policemen were beginning to take notes in the little pads of paper that they carried. The manager smiled, thinking that an arrest was imminent. "But, why?" I asked again.

"You see," he said, "in Ethiopia, especially during the long drought, we were always starving, always thirsty. We were sick from hunger and dehydration, but there was no food, little to drink, and no drugs available to cure us. Often we had to subsist on grass, and even grass became scarce. I grew up always hungry, always thirsty, always sickly, always too hot during the day, always freezing from cold during the night. But here—just look at all of this food, all of these drinks, all of this medicine. Feel the wonderful relief from the heat outside provided by the air-conditioning. When I have free time, I like to walk around stores like these simply to look at the abundance of what we have here in America. As I look around at all of this, I know that I shall never have to be so hungry again. I know that my children will not suffer from dehydration, typhus, and dysentery. I look around and I am so grateful to be here in America, a land where people do not have to starve."

The embarrassed policemen put away their pads and left.

When we take for granted what we have, the attitude of gratitude tends to be eclipsed. Here the wisdom of the medieval Hebrew adage rings true, "If you cannot have what you want, then at least want what you have." And this leads us to another level of the attitude of gratitude—being thankful for what we already have, for the blessings that we always have been granted, like food, our daily bread.

Some of what we have to be grateful for is unusual and extraordinary. Much of what we have to be grateful for is ordinary and mundane. Many religious traditions have developed sacred texts, liturgies, and rituals aimed at stimulating us to express our gratitude for what we have received, for what we partake of as part of our routine of daily living, for what we usually have enjoyed, for what we have not lacked, and consequently, for what we tend to take for granted. For example, prayers recited at mealtimes encourage us to be grateful for our daily bread, whether or not we've been deprived of it in the past. The attitude of gratitude sees food not as an entitlement, but as a gift, a blessing. These prayers remind us that each meal can become a thanksgiving dinner.

Some years ago, I was working on an interfaith prayer book on thanksgiving with a friend of mine who is a Catholic nun. The book is called *Thank God*. Our editor was pressing us to complete the manuscript and to submit it to meet the deadline. We arranged to spend a day together to prepare the final version of the book for submission. After many hours of work and many cups of coffee, my bladder was about ready to explode. I excused myself for a much needed, urgent visit to the bathroom. When I returned to our work table, much relieved, I asked my friend, "Does your tradition—Roman Catholicism—have a blessing expressing gratitude for a successful venture in the bathroom?"

She seemed somewhat surprised, if not offended by the question. At first, she thought that I was joking, but when she saw that I was serious, she thought about it for a moment and simply said, "No."

"The Lord's Prayer reminds us to ask God to 'Give us this day our daily bread,' and Jewish tradition requires us to say a blessing of gratitude to God before and after we eat," I said. "Eating food is a natural human need, but so is going to the bathroom. When unable to go, we experience considerable discomfort. Being able to relieve this discomfort should be something to be grateful for. It is worthy, therefore, of a blessing of gratitude."

I was reminded of a scene in *The Godfather, Part II* when Michael Corleone visits the gangster Hyman Roth in Miami, who is suffering from prostate cancer. I described the scene to my colleague. In great pain, Roth confesses that he'd give millions of dollars just to be able to urinate without discomfort.

"Does *your* tradition have such a blessing?" she asked.

"Yes," I answered, reciting for her.

"Praised are you, Lord our God, Creator of the universe, who with wisdom fashioned the human body, creating openings, arteries, glands, and organs, marvelous in structure, intricate in design. Should but one of them, by being blocked or open, fail to function, it would be impossible to exist. Praised are you, Lord, healer of all flesh who sustains our bodies in wondrous ways."

"I like it," she said. "Let's include it in our book." We did.

In the musical *Fiddler on the Roof*, Tevye relates that Jewish tradition has a blessing for everything. Some blessings relate to things we can be grateful to have, some to things for which we can be grateful from having been spared, and many to things that we readily take for granted until they are either withheld or are not available to us. For example, there are blessings for seeing the beauties of nature, for tasting a piece of fruit never before eaten, for awakening from a deep sleep, for smelling a pleasing fragrance, for wearing a new suit of clothes, and even for being able to go to the bathroom. Gratitude is not limited to the bold bonanzas life has to offer. Rather, the attitude of gratitude more often relates to the daily occurrences, the ordinary experiences, the most mundane activities, because those are the ones we are most likely to take for granted.

The highest level of the attitude of gratitude is spontaneous thanksgiving—reciprocating graciousness with gratitude. Try what I call the Fiddler on the Roof exercise. Think of all those you love and of all those who love you. Now think about what life would be like without them, and consequently, of how and why we should express our gratitude for their contribution to our daily lives. Think of how each moment of each day, there are so many things we take for granted that are blessings in disguise, and ponder how we can express gratitude for each of them.

Our values constitute the building blocks for creating each of our lives as works of art, and the attitude of gratitude reminds us of those people and things we value. It compels us to be consciously and continuously aware of the people, relationships, commitments, and things that imbue our lives with meaning and beauty. It cajoles us to accept what we have as a gift, as a blessing. Discovering that what is readily taken for granted is actually the miraculous in disguise draws forth humility. Gratitude helps to instill within us the conviction that something transcends us, that life is not the result of blind random forces. The attitude of gratitude teaches that it is ungracious not to be grateful, that thanksgiving is reciprocity for a grace bestowed upon us.

Though we often strive and seek to acquire material things like a new car, a new suit, or a piece of jewelry, upon deep reflection we find that these things are not what we truly value most and what we are most deeply grateful for. Rather, it is those irreplaceable relationships, convictions, and experiences that bestow meaning and significance upon our lives.

On October 3, 1789, George Washington issued a presidential proclamation establishing the Day of Thanksgiving as an everlasting holiday on the American calendar. In this document, Washington stated, "Whereas it is the duty of all nations to acknowledge the providence of Almighty God, to obey his will, to be grateful for his benefits, and humbly to implore his protection and favor—and whereas both Houses of Congress have by their joint committee requested me 'to recommend to the People of the United States a day of public thanksgiving and prayer to be observed by acknowledging with grateful hearts the many signal favors of Almighty God.' . . . Now therefore, I do recommend . . . that we may then all unite in rendering unto him our sincere and humble thanks—for his kind care and protection of the People of this country. . . ."

For George Washington, thanksgiving was ultimately a recognition of divine grace, a testimony to God's providential care, an act of reciprocity for blessings bestowed. Gratitude is a conclusion to a premise that is faith. For Washington, as for generations of Americans since his time, faith means religious faith, faith in God. Since Washington's time down to our own, the vast majority of Americans have affirmed a belief in God.

On our currency, it is written, "In God we trust." In the Pledge of Allegiance, we acknowledge that we are "one nation *under* God, indivisible, with liberty and justice for all." On many civil occasions, we sing, "Our fathers' God, to Thee, Author of liberty, to Thee we sing." Our national leaders often end their public addresses with "God bless America." Though the nature of the faith of Americans may differ, the conviction that a divine being exists characterizes the beliefs of most Americans. Opinion polls consistently find that more than 95 percent of all Americans believe in the existence of a divine being. The attitude of gratitude for many people is grounded in the belief in a God who transcends us.

For many, faith is the foundation for moral behavior. For people of faith, an answer to the question of why we should be moral is that being good is the way in which we articulate our faith as deeds. A moral act is a prayer in the form of a deed. It is an act of reciprocity for God's grace. Cultivating the moral virtues is how we try to demonstrate through action our having been created in the image of God. In the opening chapter of the Bible, God is described as surveying the world just created and seeing that "it was good." For the person of religious faith, the challenge is to correlate our actions with God's observation.

⊷

Once there were two little girls who were best friends. One was Chris-tian, the other was Jewish. After Christmas, the grandfather of the Chris-tian girl asked her, "What did your best friend get for Christmas?"

"Oh, she's not Christmas, Grandpa," the little girl replied. "I am Christmas, and she is Hanukkah." Then she paused for a moment, smiled, and said, "But we're both Thanksgiving."

7

Keep the Faith

*A person who can believe in nothing
can believe in anything.*

—G. K. CHESTERTON, BRITISH JOURNALIST AND AUTHOR

*O*nce a boy went with his father to a field to fly a kite. The boy held the rope, and the kite soared aloft. The father left for a while, and when he returned, the boy was still holding the string. Meanwhile, the kite had flown far up into the sky, so far that it was lost from sight. The father asked the boy, "Where is the kite?" "It's way above us, in the sky," said the boy. "I don't see it," said the father. "How do you know the kite is still there?" "Because," said the boy, "I feel the tug from above." Faith is feeling the tug from above.

For the person who has faith in God, and who believes that God is the source of morality, ethics is not simply a matter of opinion, emotion, or social convention. Rather, faith in God provides a compelling reason for why to be moral. For example, there is the well-known biblical teaching, "You should love your neighbor as yourself." But why should I love my neighbor? The answer comes in the rest of the verse: "I am the Lord, your God." A person should love his neighbor *because* "I am the Lord, your

God." In other words, precisely because God exists and is the author of moral norms, a person is obliged to treat himself and his neighbor in a certain way. From this perspective, a morality that is rooted in subjective human opinion rests upon a fragile foundation. Something more objective, transcendent, and lasting is required to offer a foundation for our moral convictions—and that is faith in God.

Why should we treat another human being in a certain way? The biblical answer is because we have been created in the image of God. But what is the meaning of this enigmatic Hebrew phrase *tzelem elohim*—"image of God"? It appears in the first chapter of Genesis in the story of the creation of the first human being. What do we know about God up to this point in the biblical narrative? All we know is that God is the supremely creative being. And, of all of the creatures and entities that God is described as creating, only the human creature is depicted as having been created in the image of God. We can therefore interpret the phrase "image of God" to mean that what human beings share with God is the creative ability, that like God, human beings are creative artists. For human beings to articulate the image of the divine implanted within them, they must become creative beings. Each individual must create his own life as a work of art. One way of doing this is by ethical living.

In cultivating the moral virtues, we bear witness to our having been created in God's image. Because human beings have been created in the divine image, they should try to act in godly ways. This is called *imitatio Dei* in Latin. For example, as God loves, so should we love; as God is compassionate, so should we strive for compassion; as God provides for others, so should we. This teaching does not expect us to become God. It does not ask us to be a duplicate either of God or of the moral models that we are drawn to revere. Rather, it asks us to emulate them and their virtue in the process of creating our own life as a work of art.

How we conceive of God directly affects how we express our humanity and our morality. This is why, as was mentioned before, understandings of God as a kind of celestial accountant, or as a despotic judge, or as a heavenly vending machine into which we deposit prayers and good deeds and from which we anticipate automatic rewards, are views that are both theologically and morally problematic. The alternative view, taken here, is that God is a creative artist, a loving parent, an understanding friend, a partner in the task of improving ourselves and of enhancing our world.

The person who believes in God and the person who does not so believe—the theist and the atheist (and agnostic)—disagree on the existence of God, but also on much, much more. They are divided by fundamentally different philosophies of existence, by conflicting views of the origin of the universe and the source of moral norms.

The theist's faith is grounded in the claim that God is; that the world is because God is; that there is evidence of design, purpose, and meaning in the world and in human existence; that this design and purpose are the compositions of a Designer; and that moral norms that provide human life with meaning and purpose inhere in the Designer, that is, God. The alternative to the theistic view is to affirm the existence of the universe as a sheer, unexplained brute fact. It is to posit either that the universe and human life have no intrinsic purpose or that such purpose is either merely apparent or a human contrivance, that moral norms inhere only in the precarious realm of human invention, and that the religious experience of humankind throughout the ages has been but one grand delusion.

For the theist, a reasonable means of explaining how and why we are here and what we ought to do here is available. For the nontheist, the burden of explaining how and why we are here and what the purpose is of our being here remains an open question. The theist affirms meaning, purpose, and the presence of road maps for creating the artful life, while the nontheist must discover and build a life upon his own fabrications.

Neither the theist nor the nontheist can prove the truth of his position. But the theist offers a way of explaining the universe and the human place in it. The nontheist may discard the theist's position; he may reject the theist's premises and conclusions. Nevertheless, the nontheist must do more than simply debunk the theist's view. The nontheist must establish a basis for explaining how the universe came to be, from where human purpose may be derived, and how moral norms might be discerned. For the theist, the ultimate question is how to live a life consistent with the Creator's purpose, how to create an artful existence from the life entrusted into his care. The nontheist, on the other hand, might be led to affirming with Macbeth that "Life's but a walking shadow, a poor player that struts and frets his hour upon the stage, and then is heard no more; it is a tale told by an idiot, full of sound and fury, signifying nothing."

For the theist, there is intrinsic meaning in human existence precisely because there is a God who created the world with purpose and meaning. For the nontheist, human meaning, like human life—indeed, like the universe itself—may be a product of chance, a mere accident. The following is a story by a medieval Jewish philosopher that illustrates this point.

Once a skeptic, who was also a great poet, came to visit a certain rabbi, who was also a poet. All through dinner, they debated the existence of God, but the skeptic remained unconvinced. After dinner, the rabbi showed the skeptic to the guest room. On the table next to the bed, the rabbi placed some paper, a quill, and a bottle of ink. He told the skeptic that should he wake up in the middle of the night and want to write, paper, pen, and ink were available. However, tired from the large dinner, the skeptic soon fell asleep. Soon afterward, the rabbi entered the room. On top of the pile of blank paper, the rabbi placed a new poem that he himself had written. He placed the quill across the manuscript of the poem, and he tilted the ink bottle so that some ink spilled onto the manuscript. Then he opened the window a little bit and left the room.

In the morning, the skeptic arose refreshed from a good night's sleep. Seeing the poem on the table, he immediately read it. He was delighted, for it was a beautiful poem with deep meaning. Later that morning, the rabbi and the skeptic had breakfast together. The skeptic thanked the rabbi for the poem, but the rabbi feigned ignorance. So the skeptic led the rabbi into the guest room and showed him the poem on the table. The ink bottle was still tilted and the window remained open.

"I did not write this poem," said the rabbi, "but it's clear what has happened here. While you slept, a wind came into the room, tilting the ink bottle and causing it to spill. The wind then moved the quill across the page to produce this poem."

"Things like this don't happen by chance," said the skeptic. "The poem has meaning and beauty, order and design. It expresses the will, creativity, and thought of its author."

"Then," said the rabbi, "if you cannot believe that a single poem can be composed by chance, how can you continue to believe that the entire universe came into being by chance? Don't you think that the beauty, order, and design of the universe also indicates that the universe had an author, a creator whom we call God?"

⌁

For the theist, the existence of God serves as the ultimate justification for moral behavior. The nontheist is challenged with the task of finding an alternative on which to base the claim that there is meaning to life, that the universe has a purpose, that morality is based upon something more than our opinions, feelings, or social conventions. If each person invents his own standards, then no one's is better than anyone else's; they are just different. Only if the standards by which we live derive from an objective, higher, transcendent source, can we escape the perils of "opinion ethics."

Finding a viable alternative to religious faith is not easy. For hundreds of years, many have tried, but they do not seem to have succeeded. In the 1995 movie *Tuskegee Airmen*, which was about the first African-American aviators, the character played by Laurence Fishburne says to one of his friends as they are learning how to fly warplanes, "If you don't believe in God, you'd better find a damned good substitute."

Faith in God assures us that we are not alone in the universe, that we have a divine partner, a divine friend. To have faith in God is to live in partnership with God, to work with God in the struggle for justice, peace, and holiness. Faith is a gift of God's grace, but it requires human effort to be whole. There is no faith at first sight. As the Talmud says:

If someone tells you, "I have labored but not found," do not believe him. If he says, "I have not labored, but have found," do not believe him. But, if he says, "I have labored and have found," then believe him.

Faith needs both the heart and the mind. Reason is a necessary but not a sufficient feature of faith. It is the custom of Hasidic Jews not to wear ties. When asked why this was so, a Hasid replied, "Because we do not want anything separating the heart from the head." Faith means not separating the heart from the head.

Throughout American history, we encounter the conviction that morality is ultimately rooted in faith. For example, in his Farewell Address to the Nation, issued on September 17, 1796, George Washington set down his vision for the new nation that he was so instrumental in helping to create. It is a long-standing custom for congressional representatives to gather together annually on Washington's birthday and for one of them to read this address aloud to the others.

Washington said: "Of all the dispositions and habits which lead to political prosperity, religion and morality are indispensable supports. . . . And let us with caution indulge the supposition that morality can be maintained without religion. Whatever may be conceded to the influence of refined education on minds of peculiar structure, reason and experience both forbid us to expect that national morality can prevail in exclusion of religious principle. . . ."

Here, Washington stresses the crucial role that religious faith and moral virtue must have in the life of the then nascent nation. Washington further emphasizes that morality ultimately must be grounded in faith. In a similar vein, the Declaration of Independence did not describe the government as the source of the people's inalienable human rights of life, liberty, and the pursuit of happiness. Rather, it describes these rights as having been endowed by the Creator, by God. In this view, human rights do not have their origin in human beings. Rather, they inhere in a higher, objective, transcendent source—in God.

Writing the majority opinion for the U.S. Supreme Court in the 1952 case of *Zorach v. Clausen*, Justice William Douglas wrote, "We are a religious people whose institutions presuppose a Supreme Being." Earlier that year, shortly after being elected president, Dwight D. Eisenhower said, "Our government makes little sense unless it is founded on a deeply religious faith, and I don't care what it is." Further, in 1955, President Eisenhower observed that "without God, there could be no American form of government, nor an American way of life."

Throughout history, stories about the high moral character of historical heroes have been used as a pedagogic device for teaching the moral virtues. For example, in Jewish education throughout the centuries, stories have been told of the moral virtuosity of biblical figures and of great rabbis. In Christian moral education, the lives of Jesus, the apostles, and the saints have been used to teach people how to cultivate the moral virtues. In early American education, when ethical behavior rather than professional expertise was the primary goal of the educative process, stories about the moral fortitude of the great figures of American history, like Washington and Lincoln, were part and parcel of standard school curricula. The high moral standards of historical figures were held up before us, not only for us to admire but, more important, for us to emulate.

Of Washington's life, the nineteenth-century British novelist William Makepeace Thackeray, author of the famous novel *Vanity Fair*, wrote, "A life without stain, a fame without a flaw." How many, if any, of Washington's more recent successors to the presidency could truthfully be so described? Who are the moral heroes for people to emulate today? In the presidential debates between George Bush and Michael Dukakis, the candidates fumbled for an answer when asked to name their heroes, those whose lives they found worthy of emulating.

Both Washington—who, according to the well-known legend of the cherry tree, was incapable of telling a lie—and "Honest

Abe" Lincoln—who, according to a famous story, walked many miles to return a few pennies when he had been overpaid for a job he did—were deeply religious people, though neither was very attached to a specific religious denomination. Both were convinced that moral virtue is deeply rooted in and derivative of belief in God.

Faith is not only something a person believes but also something one does. We might consider the word *faith* as a verb rather than an abstract noun. Doing godly deeds is how an individual verifies what he claims to believe in. Faith is verified not by logic but by life, that is, by living a life compatible with our stated beliefs. For instance, when someone says "I love you" to another person, the proof of the truth of the statement is not its logical validity. Rather, the proof is demonstrated in the performance of deeds that are consistent with the claim of love. In prayer, we state our faith commitment. How we act, how we live, demonstrates whether we are what we pray, whether we do what we say. To have faith means to bear witness by how we live to the presence of God in our world and in our lives. We articulate our beliefs through the lifestyle we elect to follow.

I have known many people of various faiths who have lived what they believe. One of them was Joseph Louis Bernardin, the seventh Catholic archbishop of Chicago. Cardinal Bernardin and I had worked together on a number of projects in the late 1980s and early 1990s in interreligious dialogue. When he decided to visit Israel in March 1995, he invited some of his Jewish friends to accompany him. I was proud to be among them. Our delegation of a dozen—six Catholics and six Jews—accompanied the Cardinal to meetings with Yitzhak Rabin, Yasser Arafat, and others. Together we visited places sacred to Judaism, Christianity, and Islam. We ate, laughed, talked, walked, toured, and prayed together. At Yad Va-Shem, Israel's national memorial to the Holocaust, we shed tears together. Though exhausted by our hectic schedule and constant interviews by a cadre of TV reporters who followed us to Israel from Chicago, the Cardinal was always upbeat, always asking how each of us was managing to keep up with our frantic daily schedule.

Shortly after visiting the Mount of Olives, where Jesus gave the Sermon on the Mount, the Cardinal took ill. We did not think too much of it, for within an hour he seemed better, responding to questions at a press conference in the Galilee. But this illness was a harbinger of things to come.

Cardinal Bernardin had been living under great stress in the months before the trip. In November 1993, he had been accused of sexually molesting a young man years before while he was Archbishop of Cincinnati. This young man was dying of AIDS. He tried to take away from the Cardinal his most precious possession—his personal moral integrity. Shortly before the young man died, he recanted his accusation. The Cardinal went to meet him, heard his confession, and forgave him. With this great weight lifted, Cardinal Bernardin decided to take a short respite from the crushing burden of administering the huge archdiocese of Chicago, and to do something he always had wanted to do—to visit Jesus' native land.

A few months after our return from Israel, it became known that the illness he suffered from during the trip was not sporadic. He was diagnosed with pancreatic cancer. For over a year, the surgery to remove the cancer seemed to have been effective. But in August 1996, while taking routine tests before a spinal operation aimed at relieving the terrible back pain from which he suffered because of spinal stenosis, it was discovered that the cancer had returned, that it had spread, and that it was terminal. The Cardinal called a press conference and told a stunned audience that he had less than a year to live. He had hoped to live at least until Christmas, but he did not survive even until Thanksgiving.

At the end of his life, Cardinal Bernardin wrote a book called *The Gift of Peace*. The book was completed days before his death and was published a few months later. He would have been happily surprised to see it reach the *New York Times* Bestseller List and stay on it for many weeks. Even after death, the Cardinal was able, through this book and the example of his life, to extend his pastoral ministry to hundreds of thousands of people, especially to those suffering from chronic illnesses. In his book, he describes how faith fortified his ability to deal with the false accusations against him, how it gave him courage to contend with a fatal disease, how it strengthened him to face death itself, and how his misfortunes inspired him to a greater love and empathy for others instead of making him bitter and withdrawn. From his experience, Cardinal Bernardin describes the ability to "let go" as a crucial component of faith. He says that letting go can be a liberation from self-obsession, triviality, and fear, and that it can bring about an opening of oneself to oneself and to others.

Cardinal Bernardin concluded his book with one of his favorite prayers, a prayer attributed to St. Francis of Assisi. It has become one of my favorite prayers as well. Perhaps it will also become one of yours.

↭

Lord, make me an instrument of your peace.
Where there is hatred, let me sow love.
Where there is injury, pardon.
Where there is doubt, faith.
Where there is despair, hope.
Where there is darkness, light.
Where there is sadness, joy.
Divine Master, grant that I may not so much seek
to be consoled, as to console;
to be understood, as to understand;
to be loved, as to love;
for it is in giving that we receive,
it is in pardoning that we are pardoned.
It is in dying that we are reborn to eternal life.

8

Ego Management

*An attitude of humility, of willingness to make
even the smallest contributions and to accept
a life of commitment and dedication, must be part of
the potentially creative person's way of life.*

—Psychoanalyst Silvano Arieti

*O*nce there was a construction worker who would have lunch every day with his fellow workers. Each day, he would open his lunch box, take out a baloney sandwich, and complain about having baloney again that day for lunch. Tired of listening to his daily complaint, one of his co-workers finally said to him, "If you're so tired of baloney sandwiches, why don't you ask your wife to make you something else for lunch?"

To which the worker replied, "Oh, my wife doesn't make my lunch. I do."

The moral of the story is that we feed ourselves baloney but tend to do nothing about it. And a great deal of the baloney we feed ourselves has to do with ourselves.

Strange as it may sound, people like to deceive themselves, to fool themselves into believing what they know deep down to be false. Some people deceive themselves for reasons of convenience, others to assuage feelings of guilt for doing what they know they should not be doing. Ironically, we become indignant when we realize that we have been deceived by someone else, but we seem content to live comfortably with our own proclivities to deceive our own selves. *Mundus vult decipi*, says the old Latin proverb: "The world wants to be deceived."

✦

Rabbi Bunem of Przysucha was once asked by a disciple to describe a pious person. The rabbi thought for a moment and said, "A pious person is one who does more than the law requires."

"What does the law require?"

"The law requires that a person must not deceive his neighbor," said the rabbi. "But the pious person will go beyond the requirements of the law and will not deceive his own self."

✦

Kate had been divorced for a few years when she met Andy. She was approaching 35 and was desperate to remarry and start a family. She and Andy dated for over a year. Kate helped him with his business. She loaned him money when he needed it. She arranged for vacations to exotic and romantic places, all in the hope and with the expectation that Andy would marry her. She was as generous to him in bed as she was out of bed.

Andy told her that he loved her, but his behavior indicated something very different. Kate's best friends told her that Andy was using her and that he didn't really love her. Kate responded to their observations with anger and hostility. She even severed some of her most long-standing friendships.

Eventually, Kate gave Andy an ultimatum to become engaged or to break up. Andy told her that she was unduly possessive and mentally ill. Another six months passed with Kate too afraid to confront Andy again for fear of losing him, because she really believed that she loved him and that he loved her.

One day, Andy left town for a month on an extended business trip, but he never called or wrote to Kate while he was away. When he returned, he called Kate and, with no apology, asked to see her. She agreed, thinking that he had missed her very much while they had been apart, and that he wanted to see her to tell her how much he missed and loved her. She believed he would say that while he had been away, he had thought things through and had decided that they should get married.

Andy came to Kate's house bearing beautiful roses and a silver bracelet as gifts. He took her out for a lavish dinner. Afterward, they returned to her house, where they made love the entire night. In the morning, she made him breakfast. He showered and dressed, and while eating, he told her that he had made an important decision while he had been away. Her heart raced. This, she believed, was the moment she had been waiting for, the moment that would prove that she had been right about Andy all along and that her friends had been wrong.

Andy finished his breakfast, looked at her, and said, "We've been getting very close lately—too close. I think we should lead separate lives. We can still date, but don't ever expect anything more from me."

Kate was too much in shock even to speak. Andy got up, kissed her on the cheek, and left.

After the door had closed, she began to cry uncontrollably. She lay down on the couch and managed to get some sleep. When she woke, she cried some more. The next day, she called Andy and told him that she would continue to date him. Despite what had happened, she still believed that he loved her and that he would marry her soon.

Self-deception poses a danger to our physical and psychological health. The longer a self-deception holds us in its trance, the more difficult it is to break its spell, as Kate eventually discovered. As Shakespeare insightfully observed, "Hell is truth seen too late."

One prominent form of self-deception is arrogance or unjustified pride. It is a form of self-deception because it leads us to believe that we are more accomplished, more talented, more powerful, more moral, more popular, or more attractive than we actually are. It deceives us into believing that we have few or no faults or shortcomings, that our problems are because of the faults and shortcomings of others, or that we are too perfect to have any problems. It stifles the process of moral self-improvement by deceiving us into believing that we are too good to improve. In a sense, pride blinds us when we look at ourselves because it prevents us from seeing who we truly are. It can also stifle our potential by leading us to believe that we could not possibly be better than we already are. The arrogant person is self-indulged and self-deluded. While constantly finding fault with others, he remains oblivious to his own shortcomings.

The opposite of pride is not humility but self-depreciation. Like pride, self-depreciation is also self-deluding. While pride is self-deceptive because it leads us to think that we are more than we are, self-depreciation is self-deceptive because it asserts that we are less than we actually are. Like pride, it cripples our ability to realize our potential by diminishing our faith in our own capabilities. In self-depreciation, people sell themselves short. Such people either fail to try or try to fail in order to reinforce their deflated view of their own selves.

Both those who inflate as well as those who deflate themselves tend to mock or to demean others both for their accomplishments and for their failings. The arrogant person will put down others in order to reassure himself of his alleged superiority over others. The self-depreciating person will demean others in an often futile attempt to establish his own self-worth. A balance is needed between these two undesirable approaches to ego management. Humility is the "golden mean" between the extremes of arrogance and self-depreciation.

Humility is often misunderstood. Many see it as a weakness, though it actually is a strength. It is a virtue, not a vice. Humility does not entail a denial or a depreciation of our own abilities and accomplishments. It does not require deluding ourselves about our real capabilities. Rather, humility means acknowledging our talents and our accomplishments but not exaggerating their significance. Humility asks us to make a candid appraisal of our superior abilities when compared to others, but it also demands that we undertake an exercise in rigorous self-scrutiny regarding our insufficiencies when compared to the abilities and achievements of others. It cajoles us to strive to correct our faults so that we might improve ourselves.

Humility leads us to a forthright awareness of our limitations. This can become a source of power rather than weakness. Candidly confronting our limitations should not be viewed as an exercise in closing possibilities, but as one of clarifying options. Only when we are aware of what we cannot do, or of what we can no longer do—for example, because of physical limitations due to age—can we begin to focus on what we can realistically expect to accomplish. It would be foolish to expect to become an opera star if you were a monotone. Similarly, an unathletic person cannnot realistically anticipate winning Olympic medals. Accepting our limitations is not a confession of failure but an act of inner liberation. Once people know what they cannot do, they become free to set out on the path of accomplishing what they can do, of becoming who they can become. Two critical components of humility are the recognition of limitations and the actualization of potentiality.

Humility is often considered to be an enemy of real self-esteem. But it is not. Humility embraces authentic self-esteem but has little tolerance for counterfeit self-esteem. For instance, self-esteem becomes self-deceptive and counterfeit when it is based upon expectations that underestimate our capabilities or that overestimate our achievements. Pride and self-deception inevitably lead us to false self-esteem. As the great American pragmatic philosopher William James pointed out over a century ago, authentic self-esteem depends upon the ratio of expectation to success. For example, people who set their goals too low will inevitably experience high self-esteem, but they will relinquish the promise of living up to their potential. Such individuals will thereby surrender any possibility of achieving excellence in their endeavors. What is achieved is not really self-esteem but self-delusion.

Much of American education has adopted the view that the purpose of the educational process is to allow the student to feel good about himself, to experience self-esteem. As a result, the failing grade has been eliminated in many school systems because failing a course would harm a student's self-esteem. No matter if the student never learns to read, write, or add. Many schools have gone even further and have abolished grades altogether because bad grades would make mediocre and poor students stop liking themselves. Consequently, intellectually precocious students are actively discouraged from developing their abilities, lest their achievements make their classmates feel bad about themselves. Such an approach is dangerous because it stifles the quest for excellence.

In my view, this approach is destroying our educational institutions and, consequently, is weakening us as a nation. Further, this is happening at precisely the time when we need to encourage excellence in education. Despite the widespread assumption that self-esteem is a necessary prerequisite for academic success, there is not a single study that demonstrates that claim to be true. Studies consistently show that the result of focusing education on the student's perceived need to feel good about himself has resulted in what has been called the dumbing down of the curriculum and the collapse of academic standards in many American schools. Indeed, a study reported in the journal *Psychological Review* found that a false sense of high self-esteem can lead to greater violence than a sense of low self-regard. Individuals who have an unrealistically inflated image of themselves are inevitably threatened by those who offer a more accurate portrait of objective reality.

Authentic self-esteem is for those who have achieved more than they expected to achieve, who have raised their goals a notch higher than their expectations, and who have met that self-imposed challenge. Authentic self-esteem is based upon real humility, which means recognizing our strengths as a prelude to confronting our weaknesses and to improving in the areas where we are not as strong.

Humility means accepting yourself for who you are and striving to develop yourself into who you can yet become. A characteristic of both the self-aggrandizer and the self-deprecator is that neither wants to be who they really are, which is proven by the fact that each avoids a candid self-appraisal of who they are. The enterprise of crafting one's life into a work of art begins with an honest evaluation of the raw materials with which each of us has to work. This process begins with self-knowledge—with a forthright awareness of our abilities and limitations, accomplishments and defeats. The first step in ego management is to tear down the cobwebs of self-deception woven by either undue self-aggrandizement or by self-depreciation. Only then can a person proceed with the challenge at hand. Only then can one truly affirm "I wanna be me."

The prideful person devoid of humility tends to see everything and everyone in the world either as an extension of his ever-expanding ego or as part of a plot against him. In other words, paranoia goes hand in hand with pride. For example, when such a person watches a football game, he assumes that when the team goes into a huddle, they are talking about him. While this example is an exaggeration, it nonetheless describes a kind of behavior that reminds me of Hal.

Hal is a former student of mine who is a clergyman. When he was first ordained, I would call him every few months to see how he was faring in his ministry at his first congregation. I would always begin the conversation by asking, "How are you and the family?" Hal would respond by saying something like, "My wife, my daughters, my son, and my dog are fine. My congregation loves me and bought me a new car. The house they provide for me is a $350,000 house. Five hundred fifty people came to services last week to hear me preach, and 150 came to my lecture at the local college."

It took me a while to catch on to the fact that when Hal tells me how many people came to hear him speak, this is his way of answering my question about how he is. The more people who come, the better he is—because he assumes that they come to services only to hear his words of wisdom. It does not occur to him that they might be coming to pray. One time, I called Hal and he was depressed. Only 150 people had come to services that weekend. No matter that his area was hit that weekend by the biggest snowfall in 50 years.

Whenever I speak to Hal, I am always surprised by how many times he uses first-person pronouns, like "I," "me," or "mine." Hal is not aware of it, but his problem with ego management may indicate a future problem with health management.

When you go for a medical checkup, the doctor will often measure your blood pressure and your cholesterol to detect present or potential heart disease. But have you ever gone for a checkup where the physician listens to you talk and counts how many times you use first-person pronouns like "I," "me," or "mine" in order to determine the probable health of your heart?

A long-term study of 600 men was conducted by Professor Larry Scherwitz, a University of California psychologist. He found that among the men he studied, those who most often used the first-person pronouns had the highest risk of heart trouble. After following his subjects for several years, he found that the more habitually a man talked about himself, the greater the chance he would have a coronary. He discovered that self-obsession may be a greater catalyst for the onset of heart disease than smoking, improper diet, or lack of exercise. His findings confirm the view that links the health of the soul to the health of the body, that claims that the cultivation of the moral virtues—in this case, humility—has a direct impact upon our physical well-being, upon our total health.

Hal's clerical colleagues in the city where he lives find his egocentricity so overt as to be almost humorous. One of them told me that at meetings, they tease him by saying things like, "When Hal travels by plane, he needs to buy two tickets—one for himself and one for his ego." But Hal's situation isn't funny; it's tragic and self-destructive. He keeps tripping over his own ego as he tries to do things. For instance, he has problems forging lasting and intimate relationships because he tends to see people either as extensions of his ego or as potential assailants upon his puffed-up portrait of himself.

Hal's first marriage worked as long as his wife, Ellen, catered to his every whim, constantly praised his every achievement, and supported his every activity—even when they were manipulative and wrong. Ellen passively accepted Hal's every scowl and his constant outbursts against all those whom he believed were "out to get him." But after 10 years of marriage and two children,

Ellen no longer wanted to remain Hal's "extension cord"—as she called it. She went back to school, earned a degree, found a job, and began to develop her own identity. Hal refused to tolerate it. In his mind, Ellen already had an identity. She was an adjunct of his ego. The marriage began to deteriorate. Meanwhile, Hal was also having trouble at work.

At rites of passage at which he officiated, Hal always thrust himself onto center stage—and people began to notice and resent it. At weddings, he would dress up to the hilt and loudly ask people how he looked, thereby trying to divert attention from the bride and groom. At funerals, he would deliver eulogies aimed at drawing people's attention to his oratorical skills rather than to the virtues of the deceased. After a funeral, he would encourage the attendees to congratulate him for his eulogy rather than comforting the mourners present.

Hal desperately wanted the approval of others, though he saw offering his approval of others as somehow being a diminution of himself. Because of his consuming need to be loved, he would pretend to agree with everybody—lest they not love him. He would promise to do things for people to evoke their instant appreciation and admiration, but when doing what he promised turned out not to be to his advantage, he would fail to follow through on what he promised. Eventually, all these things caught up with him, and he had indications that he would soon be fired from his job.

Hal blamed all of his difficulties on Ellen, claiming that she had abandoned him in his time of need. He divorced her. Before the ax fell at work, he took a position at a larger and wealthier congregation across the country. He became increasingly alienated from his children, whom he left behind. Before long, he met someone else, remarried, and the cycle started all over again.

At his new congregation, Hal adopted a new strategy. He pretended to be overly pious and humble. He practiced a false humility. He epitomized what a medieval theologian called pride in humility. In other words, he paraded his humility around in a constant public display so that people would talk about how humble, pious, and moral he was. When people asked him to do things he was capable of doing, but that he did not want to do because he saw no personal advantage to doing them, he feigned piety—"I have to pray"; or he took a humble posture—"God has not given me the ability to take on such a great challenge." Hal was quickly becoming Machiavelli's model of a leader—a person who is not virtuous but who works hard to *appear* to be virtuous so that he can use the appearance of propriety to manipulate the behavior of others for his own advantage.

At Hal's new congregation, there was a teacher in the religious school who had been there for many years. She was beloved by all the people of the congregation. She was dedicated, hard-working, and effective. She threw her entire being into her work. Hal couldn't stand it because he wanted everyone there to love him the way they loved her. So he began to circulate rumors that she was sexually abusing the schoolchildren, and a few months later, he fired her. She sued. At the trial, the truth came out. As a result, Hal was discharged. She was completely vindicated, but because suspicions lingered, her career and her life were ruined. She was another victim of Hal's egocentricity. Hal took another position, and the cycle began all over again.

To this day, Hal has not yet realized how his ego gets in his way, how it restricts his ability to develop his innate talents, how it stifles his attempts to develop authentic and intimate relationships. Philosopher Bertrand Russell said, "Too powerful an ego is a prison from which to escape." But Hal remains imprisoned within his egocentricity. Unbridled pride is not only self-deceptive but also self-destructive. As Scripture teaches, "Pride precedes destruction and a haughty spirit goes before a fall."

Though he is constantly surrounded by people, Hal is often lonely and frequently depressed. Long before contemporary psychoanalysts such as Heinz Kohut identified depression as a symptom both of self-depreciation and of arrogance, this insight was already taught by mystical masters. In this view, arrogance and self-depreciation are two sides of the same coin of egocentricity. Both manifest themselves in psychological depression. What the self-depreciating person and the arrogant person have in common is that they are both self-obsessed—the self-depreciating person with how tragic his life is, the arrogant person with how extraordinarily perfect he is. In both of these forms of egocentricity, the individual focuses constantly and exclusively on himself. Such people speak of themselves incessantly—the arrogant person continuously boasting, the self-depreciating person always deflating himself and blaming others for his tragic lot in life. Both types of behavior engender depression. Both types of individuals tend to manifest their insecurities through anger.

The paradox of anger is that while focusing on the ego, it can cause one to lose control of one's self. The arrogant person is often characterized as one who scowls angrily at others, especially those who do not adequately take notice of his presumed, but often illusory, greatness. The self-depreciating person tends to be angry both at himself for not being what he wants to be, and at others for allegedly sabotaging his efforts to do what he wants to do. As Benjamin Franklin said, "Anger is never without reason, but seldom a good one."

While anger is sometimes justified, habitual anger is a toxic emotion. It elevates the risk of many diseases, including heart disease. When manifested as prolonged depression, it can become a serious danger to our health. Carried too far, anger and depression are suicidal, either in the short or long term—in the short term as an act of desperation, in the long term as an emotional state that weakens not only our natural immunities to a variety of diseases but which also hampers the pumping efficiency of our hearts. Contrary to popular opinion, it is not the workaholic who finds meaning in his work who is really at risk. Rather, it is the person whose life is heavily punctuated with outbursts of anger, hostility, and rage who is endangered. Furthermore, anger is not only dangerous to the individual who perpetuates it, but it is harmful to others as well. Anger is especially devastating because what it destroys cannot be readily restored.

Still another common characteristic of the arrogant and the self-depreciating person is his obsession with how others view him. His ego cannot permit him a moment's rest because of his concern about being scrutinized and judged by others. Neither type of person is primarily motivated by what is good or true, but rather by how things look. Always opting for appearance over reality, he conspires with himself to deceive not only his own self, but others as well. The arrogant person wants to gain approval in order to reinforce his deluded view of his own exaggerated aura of self-importance. The self-depreciating person sadistically enjoys being put down and putting others down in order to wallow in his misery. Every time I see Hal, he asks me, "Well, how do I look? How am I doing? What do people think of me?" But Hal couldn't take the truth. One time, I simply said, "Hal, why are you always so preoccupied with how you look? Maybe no one is looking."

The spiritual maestros of past generations prescribed three antidotes to arrogance. The first is the contemplation of the reality of our own mortality. Thinking about the inevitability of death is intended to jolt us away from our habitual tendency to place undeserved importance on the superficial trappings of everyday life instead of focusing on the fragility of life and the consequential importance of living a life that matters. In Thornton Wilder's play *Our Town*, a person who has died is allowed to return to live one day of her life again. Later, she regrets the decision. While she cherishes the preciousness of each moment of that day and the joy of being reunited with those she loved, those around her are preoccupied with squabbling over silly issues, holding grudges for nonsensical reasons, being angry for not getting adequate attention, and obsessing on transient and whimsical needs. Seeing life from the perspective of its finitude offers us a potent reason for putting the ego aside to attend to the task of meaningful living, to the crafting of life as a work of art.

The second age-old antidote to arrogance is contemplation of the vicissitudes of life. For example, the wealthy person can become arrogant, led to believe by himself and others that because he has so much, he is so much. But knowing that life is like an ever-rotating wheel, he can be brought to realize that the rich may become poor, the powerful subservient, the famous obscure, the healthy ill. As the nineteenth-century American journalist Horace Greeley put it, "Fame is a vapor, popularity an accident, riches take wings; only one thing endures, and that's character."

The third part of the ancient prescription against arrogance is the cultivation not only of humility but of equanimity. Etymologically related to the word *equal*, equanimity means trying to take all things as being equal, without being overly impressed or depressed by them. The person who has achieved equanimity takes things in stride. The harsh and unjustified criticism and disapproval of others will not rattle him. Inevitable frustrations and setbacks will not fluster him. The exaggerated praise of others will not impress him. He proceeds on an even keel, unperturbed by annoyances or applause, in the pursuit of a life of excellence, meaning, and goodness.

It is told that when the Finnish composer Sibelius visited Germany, he was shown statues and monuments of great German composers like Mozart and Beethoven. He turned to his guide and said, "You know, it's interesting; composers tend to worry all the time about what the critics will say about their work, yet I have never seen a statue or a monument dedicated to even a single critic. I think I'll concentrate on composing the best music I can and not worry so much about what the critics will say—and my music will be the better for it."

Humility is considered a virtue, partly because it is a vital component of purposeful and creative activity. The truly creative person knows that setting aside the ego is necessary for the creative process to proceed unhampered by one's being overly self-conscious. Such a person realizes that the ego can serve as the greatest obstacle to free creative expression. For example, in an interview, the great tenor Luciano Pavarotti said that if he thinks about what the critics might say while he is singing, he becomes too preoccupied to be able to hit the high notes. Only when he forgets about what the critics might say can he sing his best and can his true artistic self emerge. Great athletes know that focusing on the ego, worrying about whether they will perform as expected when at play, is the surest predictor of failure. As Yogi

Berra said about baseball, "You can't hit and think at the same time." The same is true of other areas of attainment.

When discussing self-deception a few pages ago, I quoted one of my favorite sages, the nineteenth-century Hasidic master Rabbi Bunem of Przysucha. He has insightful advice about how to manage the ego.

❖

In the Bible it is written, "I am but dust and ashes." And in the Talmud it is written, "Each person should say: For me the world was created." Now a person should always wear a garment with two pockets. In one pocket, he should place a slip of paper on which it is written, "I am dust and ashes." In the other pocket, he should place a slip of paper on which it is written, "For me the world was created." He should pull out the appropriate slip when he needs it.

When he is puffed up with pride, he should take out and read the slip that says, "I am dust and ashes" and contemplate its meaning, and his arrogance should vanish. When he feels depreciated and depressed, he should pull out the other slip of paper and read, "For me the world was created" and contemplate its meaning, and his depression should vanish. His sense of self-worth should be replenished.

In either case, when a person's balance has been restored, he can go back to the lifelong task of creating life as a work of art.

9

Watch Your Words

Why do ears have lobes?
So that when we anticipate hearing evil speech,
we can place the lobe over the ear's entrance
to prevent such words from entering.

—RABBINIC SAYING

*T*here's a story about a rabbi, a priest, and a minister in a certain town who became friends. Often, they would go places together and talk about their common experiences as clergy.

One day, they went fishing together, and the minister said to his colleagues, "We've been friends for years, and we have no one else in town to talk to about certain things. Confession is good for the soul, but we have no one to whom to confess our faults and shortcomings. So maybe today, each of us should confess our most secret sins and faults to one another."

They agreed, and the Catholic priest began, "I have tried to the best of my ability to be a good priest and pastor to my flock these many years, and I think I've done a good job. But I am still a man with wants and urges, and occasionally my vow of chastity weighs heavily upon me. So every few months I tell the people in my parish that I am going on a spiritual retreat, but, in fact, I drive to a town in the neighboring state where I spend a few days in a certain bordello. Then I return here better able to fulfill my priestly duties."

The minister went next, and he said, "You know, they don't pay me very much, and with my kids at college, I have more expenses and debts than I can handle. So, every week, I take a few dollars from the collection plate or from petty cash for personal day-to-day expenses. A little bit here and a little bit there, things add up, and I'm able to make ends meet. I know it's wrong, but I can't help myself."

It was now the rabbi's turn, but he was hesitant to speak. His colleagues pressed him not to be shy, not to be afraid or reluctant. They assured him that they were his colleagues, his friends, and that they would understand—whatever his confession might reveal.

Finally, the rabbi said, "I have many faults—but my greatest shortcoming is that I am an uncontrollable gossip. And while the two of you were talking, I was thinking about how I can't wait to get back to town to tell everyone what you've each just told me."

✣

I had a friend and colleague named Laura. She is a very devout Christian. She was a member of the faculty of a theological seminary run by the denomination to which she belongs. We met through a mutual colleague, who recommended that she consult me about her doctoral dissertation which she was then just beginning to research and write. It was on a topic in which I have some expertise. She came to my office to see me, and we both knew a friendship was in the making. We had many interests in common. We even shared certain health problems. I learned many things from her, and she from me. We simply enjoyed each other's company. We usually met for lunch or in a variety of libraries where each of us would go to do our research. As time went on, we learned a great deal about each other's private lives. She was married to a minister for many years, but they apparently could not have children. So they adopted two children from Third World countries.

Laura and her husband, Bob, are paradigms of Christian charity and virtue. They help the unemployed find jobs. They shelter abused people in their own home until another remedy can be found. They counsel distraught teenagers from committing suicide and self-abuse. Yet Laura and Bob both know that even a hint of impropriety regarding either of them could destroy both their ministries and their lives, which for them is the same thing.

One day, Laura and I met for lunch in the student cafeteria at her seminary. Though Laura is a very attractive woman, on that particular day she was resplendent. After we had taken our food and checked out with the cafeteria cashier, she led me to a table in a deserted corner, smiled, blushed, and said, "After all these years, it has finally happened. I'm pregnant. Bob and I, with the Lord's help and blessing, will have a child. In more than 20 years of marriage, it never happened before, though we never did anything to prevent it from happening. I'm so happy!"

"Thank God," I said.

Because she was already past 40, Laura had to undergo many tests—all of which showed that the baby she so joyously carried was healthy. She began to redecorate her house for the expected arrival.

Weeks passed and I did not hear from Laura. I assumed that she was too busy going to doctors, rearranging her house, and keeping up with her work to see me. Then, one day, I was in a library, looking for a book in the stacks, when I saw Laura sitting in a study carrel not far away. Her back was toward me, and she seemed to be reading. I approached her from behind and whispered, "How's Mommy?"

She turned and stood up. She looked horrible, drained.

"What's wrong, Laura?"

Tears cascaded down her ashen face.

"I lost the baby. God's will be done. But, why?"

There are situations in which anything we say, no matter how wise or profound, seems trite. This was one of them. I just took her in my arms and kissed her forehead while she cried.

After a while, she said, "I can't cry at home. I have to be strong for Bob and the children. I come here to cry and to mourn the child I've always dreamed about, who now I will never know."

In the weeks that followed that meeting, there was no word from Laura. My phone messages went unanswered. She was not to be found in the places we usually met. Finally, I wrote her a note, asking how she was. A few days later, she called. Her tone was curt and businesslike. She offered to meet me at a restaurant in the suburbs, far away from where either of us either lived or worked. I did not ask why. I agreed, and we met.

I hardly recognized her. It was almost as if she did not want to be recognized, as if she were incognito. She was unusually nervous, fidgety. We were seated in the restaurant. We ordered and were served, but she did not eat.

"Someone saw you hug me in the library," she said. "Rumors that we are having an affair have started to circulate. I've resigned from the seminary. I can't see you anymore. It's too risky. I have too much to lose. Bob and I have too much at stake. We've lost enough already."

From beneath the dark sunglasses she was wearing on that cloudy day, tears flowed.

"Excuse me, I have to go. Goodbye."

Laura got up and left. I have not seen her since. Our precious friendship had been severed by a member of the library staff who, misinterpreting what he saw, began to spread rumors about Laura and me.

Laura was too depleted from the loss of the baby to confront the rumors. She surrendered, realizing there was little she could do. Perhaps she was right. But I could not let things rest. I found out which librarian had started the rumors, and I confronted him. I explained the situation to him: Laura's pregnancy, the loss of the baby, the reason for my gesture, the nature of my friendship with

Laura, the damage he had done by spreading malicious gossip. As I spoke, he became visibly upset. Whether it was because he was afraid of losing his job or because he was sincerely contrite, I do not know.

"What can I do? How can I make amends?" he asked.

"That's the point. You can't. The damage has been done and is beyond repair." I left.

My friendship with Laura was hijacked because of baseless rumors. Though I lost a friend, I could have lost much more, and Laura could have, too. It happened to me. It could happen to you. It could happen to anyone.

To protect the value of your belongings, there are insurance policies and security systems. To guard against certain diseases, there are inoculations and drugs. But how can you protect yourself against rumor or innuendo? How can you protect your reputation against malicious gossip? If a person assaults you, you can defend yourself. But if people talk about you behind your back, what remedy do you have? How can a good name that has been besmirched by unsubstantiated rumors be restored?

Precisely because words have power, people should watch what they say. As the biblical book of Proverbs teaches us, "Life and death are in the power of the tongue." The ancient rabbis pointed out that though the tongue is probably our weakest organ or limb, it can nonetheless cause more damage and bring more benefits than other stronger organs and limbs. Words can hurt as well as heal. They can abuse or endear, evoke violence or tenderness. Words can deform or form relationships. They can erect barriers or open windows.

Slander and gossip may be considered a form of robbery because they can rob a person of their reputation or their integrity. Indeed, Jewish law considers slander, gossip, and verbal deception to be worse than stealing because when an item is stolen, there is always the possibility of recovering it or of financially compensating the owner for its loss. But in various types of verbal abuse, restitution is not always possible. Once a reputation has been besmirched, it is nearly impossible for it to be restored. Suspicions always linger. Words *can* hurt us.

⇲

Paul went to the best schools and graduated from Harvard Law School near the top of his class. Rather than taking a job with a prestigious law firm, he became an attorney for an advocacy group for the poor. His parents could not forgive him for not pursuing a lucrative law practice. They wanted him to marry into "the right family," but he married a wonderful woman from a poor family of immigrants. At his wedding, his mother said to him in front of his bride and his friends, "I never should have had you. I should have had an abortion instead."

⇲

The damage done by a verbal assault can be more painful and last longer than the harm caused by a physical assault. How and why a person uses words reveals a great deal about a person's character, values, and nature. The use of language is a peculiarly human characteristic. Our words articulate what kind of human beings we are, what kind of human beings we want to become, and whether we are accelerating or retarding the creation of our lives as works of art.

⇲

A bride and groom were married, exchanging wedding vows. The next morning, after a wedding night filled with passion, the bride awoke to find her husband packing his suitcase.
"Where are you going?" she asked.
"I'm leaving you."
"But yesterday at our wedding, each of us took a vow."
"Just words," he said, and then finished packing and left.

⇲

"It's all just semantics," one of my students said, commenting on a discussion on ethical problems in one of my classes.
I took out my wallet and removed a dollar bill.

"Can you give me a check for one dollar in exchange?" I asked.

"Sure," he said.

I gave him the dollar bill, and he gave me the signed check. I took my pen and added the word "hundred" after "one" on the check, and I added two zeros to the number one.

"What are you doing?" he asked angrily.

"Semantics," I answered.

⊷

If words had no meaning, the student would have no right to be angry and the bride would have no right to feel humiliated. Many people mistakenly believe that "words are cheap." A wrong word or phrase, however, can end up costing a great deal.

According to the Talmud, a slanderer is worse than a murderer. A murderer kills one person in a violent act, but a verbal abuser can destroy three people: the person who says it, the one who hears it, and the person about whom it is said. Even when it isn't slanderous or false, gossip can be harmful to reputations and to relationships. What is heard can always be misinterpreted.

There are things that should not be said, and there are things that should not be heard. Unlike other organs, the ears are open; what enters cannot readily leave. Slander and gossip enter the open ear like a virus that infects us. What is one to do? We should try to avoid hearing what should not be heard. Similarly, we should avoid saying what should not be said. As a medieval ethical treatise reminds us, we have two eyes, two ears, and two nostrils, but only one mouth. This should teach us that we should speak less than we see, hear, or smell.

Like me, you probably know heavy drinkers who can go a day without taking a drink and heavy smokers who can go a day without smoking, but how many people that you know can go a day without gossip, without saying something or listening to something—especially something negative—about someone who is not present when it is said?

If there were a pill that people could take that would prevent them from gossiping, I doubt that many would avail themselves of it. Why? Because people like to gossip. Gossip is alluring. It is verbal voyeurism. Gossip makes people feel good. It provides psychological gratification by making us feel superior to others. It elevates us by lowering the reputation of someone else. This is why people especially enjoy hearing rumors, gossip, and "news" about the private problems of the rich, the powerful, and the famous. It takes them "down a peg." Often, when we speak ill of someone else, it is our way of punishing them for having what we do not have and for being what we seem unable to become. Gossip is sometimes a way in which we seek to injure someone with whom we are angry—either for right or wrong reasons— but whom we are too timid to confront directly. Gossip demeans both ourselves and others. It can only harm, not help.

Flattery is a form of verbal abuse people love to hear. We tend not to think of flattery as verbal abuse, but it often is. Experience has taught me that when a person begins a conversation with me by saying, "Since the last time I saw you, you look like you've lost weight," this attempt at flattery will probably soon be followed by the request for a favor. When an acquaintance or co-worker calls me and begins the conversation with effusive praise of something I have done, I always expect a request soon to follow, and my prediction is rarely mistaken. Flattery is a strategy that is commonly used by people who want to manipulate someone into doing something for them that they probably do not really want to do. As Benjamin Franklin warns us, "The same man cannot be both friend and flatterer." Like gossip, flattery is seductive. We like to be flattered. As Franklin further wrote, "A flatterer never seems absurd; the flattered always takes his word."

Sometimes we say too much. Other times we do not say what needs to be said. Later, we regret not having said it. In this regard, I remember something a rabbinic colleague of mine once told me. He had recently officiated at the funeral of a woman whose husband was inconsolable in his grief. She had been terminally ill for a long time, and after she died, her husband just fell apart. At their daughter's request, the rabbi visited the widower.

"I understand your grief," said the rabbi, himself a widower. "You have had a long time to prepare for your wife's death. You took good care of her during her illness. You were with her to the end. You were a good husband. Why do you feel so guilty? Why are you still so depressed?"

"You don't understand," the man said. "I loved my wife."

"I know," said the rabbi, "but your grieving is harming your life, your health, your family, and your career. Your wife wouldn't have wanted it this way."

"You don't understand," the man said again. "I loved my wife."

"I know you did. You always will. And you miss her. But you can't continue on this way," the rabbi said.

"You don't understand," the man said. "I loved my wife—and once, I almost told her."

How many times have we *almost* said "I love you" to someone we love? How many times have we *almost* asked forgiveness when we were wrong? How many times have we *almost* said "Thank you" when we have had something to be grateful for? How many times have we *almost* said "Can I help you?" to someone in need?

Like this widower, many people are reticent to articulate their gentler emotions, but they may not hesitate to express their more base emotions, like anger, hate, and arrogance. People who find it difficult to express tenderness can become incredibly articulate when it comes to verbalizing well-targeted barbs aimed at hitting a person—especially a spouse, child, friend, or colleague—in his most vulnerable spot.

The cultivation of moral virtues such as empathy, love, and humility are potent antidotes to the destructive ravages of moral vices such as unjustified anger, apathy, and arrogance. Healing words and gestures can serve as the ambassadors of these virtues. For example, dispelling arrogance and cultivating humility are the necessary prerequisites for asking for forgiveness and for encouraging reconciliation in a severed or damaged relationship. Arrogance stifles us, whereas humility encourages us to admit, "I was wrong. I know I hurt you. I am sorry. Please forgive me." Arrogance builds a wall; humility opens a door. Anger restricts us, but love opens us up to admit, "Simply because I love you so much, I can't stay angry at you." Apathy closes us off; empathy opens us up to honestly admitting that "I really do care." Care leads to cure. The old adage "Confession is good for the soul" rings true, but only when confession is the prelude to a lasting reconciliation, to a healing. The cultivation of the moral virtues refuses to allow us to be shut up in ourselves, shut off from others, imprisoned in a maze of anger, resentment, depression, and anxiety.

Anger, apathy, arrogance, and harsh words can hurt us and others. But even the truth can hurt. In the John Candy film *Only the Lonely*, the mother of the character played by John Candy always likes to "tell it like it is," especially when she knows it will upset and humiliate someone. She uses "the truth" to manipulate those around her. In one scene, John Candy, who has been a bachelor for many years and who lives with his mother, finally falls madly in love. He brings his girlfriend home to meet his mother. Rather than sharing her son's happiness, her only concern is herself—if he marries his girlfriend, he will move out of the house and she will have to live alone. Instead of making the already nervous girlfriend feel welcome, she insults her in a brutal way because she "always tells it like it is." Finally, the girlfriend runs out of the room, crying and humiliated.

The poet William Blake reminds us that:
A truth that's told with bad intent
Beats all the lies you can invent.

My son has a friend named Tony. At 14, Tony was barely five feet tall. All his friends were much taller. One day, Tony went to the doctor for a routine checkup. All he was concerned about was how tall he would be, so he asked the doctor. Preoccupied with getting to his next patient, the doctor said, "Maybe an inch or two taller than you are now." Tony was devastated, and he went into a depression for many months. Both his schoolwork and his social life suffered tremendously. Since it's highly unlikely that the doctor could be that precise to the inch about Tony's growth, he should have just said, "You're still growing," which would have been a perfectly honest reply.

Suddenly, the following spring, Tony had a growth spurt, which ended his depression. Today, Tony is of average height and is very happy about it. He has another doctor, and he is happy about that, too.

In chapter 1, I told you about an encounter I had on a beach in Florida. Should I have told the truth to the little boy I met there? Should I have let him know that I am not Santa Claus? Should I have been cruel and truthful rather than kind? The philosopher Immanuel Kant would have told me to tell the truth no matter what. According to Kant and to many other philosophers and theologians, telling the truth is an unbreakable absolute moral rule. Lying is always wrong. A person who lies is a liar who cannot be trusted once he has broken the rule that one must always tell the truth. But is Kant right? Should a person tell the truth all the time, to everyone, in all situations?

Kant gives the following example. Suppose a person is being pursued by a would-be murderer. The person takes refuge in your house to hide so that he will not be killed. The would-be murderer comes to you and asks if his intended victim is hiding in your house. What do you tell him? Do you tell the truth, thereby putting a person's life at risk, even though a lie could save that person's life? Kant says that you should tell the truth. He says that you shouldn't lie, no matter what.

During World War II, the French philosopher Jean-Paul Sartre was involved in an actual situation similar to the theoretical one described by Kant. Sartre was involved in the French underground against the Nazis. A member of the underground was caught and interrogated by the Gestapo. The man was tortured to reveal the whereabouts of his fellow members of the French underground, but he lied. According to Kant, he should have told them the truth, even though it would have led to the roundup and execution of his colleagues. Sartre, however, disagreed. For Sartre, the captured man did the right thing by lying to save his colleagues from exposure, torture, and death. To save another person from harm, it would be right to lie.

The Talmudic rabbis also disagree with Kant. The following problem, for example, is posed in the Talmud. Suppose you are at a wedding. The bride is standing nearby. Someone asks you, "Isn't the bride beautiful?" Actually, she is quite ugly. What do you say? Do you tell the truth and traumatize the bride at her wedding in front of her groom, family, and friends, or do you lie to preserve her dignity? According to the Talmudic rabbis, this is an example of a situation in which a person is morally obliged to lie so as to save someone from humiliation, harm, or trauma. (Of course, one of the commentaries says that to say an ugly bride is beautiful is really not a lie since "beauty is in the eye of the beholder" and to her groom she inevitably would be beautiful!) Similarly, in a case where someone would be placed in mortal danger because of not lying, as in the case of the intended murder victim discussed above, telling the truth would not be the right thing to do. From this perspective, truth is important, but it is not of supreme importance. There are occasions when it should be set aside.

The Talmudic rabbis would probably have condoned my conversation with the little boy on the beach. They taught that it is wrong to lie, but they also taught that there are sometimes situations where it is more important to be kind than to be truthful, to express care rather than candor, and empathy rather than accuracy.

According to the Talmudic rabbis, what we say and how we act ought to be governed by the principle that a person's "outside should be like his inside," that a person's actions should articulate his character. From this perspective, kindness and consideration toward others is more important than always telling the truth. The reason why it is important to tell the truth is not because it is the truth, but because lying can be a way of manipulating or hurting another person. For this reason, when the truth can be used to harm someone else, it may be set aside. In such cases, silence or a "white lie" is preferable. Paradoxically, the reason we should always strive to tell the truth is the same reason the truth may sometimes be set aside, and that reason is that speech and action should not be used to intentionally harm or manipulate someone else.

Kant was only half right. He was right when he said, "Don't lie." He wasn't right when he added, "No matter what." Lying is wrong because it is deceptive and manipulative. It's dangerous not only for the person who is lied to but also for the person who lies. And it can easily become a habit. It's often easier to lie for the sake of expediency or to avoid risking the displeasure of someone else than to have to deal with the truth. But, in the long run, if we learn to lie, we lose our grasp on the truth. We surrender our integrity, our credibility. Our outside is no longer like our inside. We find it increasingly difficult to tell the truth, even when we want to do so. We lose the trust of others, and trust is the basic lubricant of all human relationships. A person who is not known to be truthful is suspected of telling a lie even when he is telling the truth.

Telling the truth is a matter of integrity. Integrity means that a person's actions and words express his character, that he is who he says, that his words articulate his commitments, and that his inside is the same as his outside. To put it simply: A person is as good as his word. The corollary is also true: A word is as good as its person. The great American novelist Jack London warned us to use words carefully, as if each cost us $1,000.

Creating life as a work of art requires the cultivation of moral virtues such as integrity, kindness, care, and truthfulness. But, as the New Testament reminds us, "In the beginning, there was the word" (John 1:1).

Once it happened that in a small Eastern European town, a man who was jealous of the town's rabbi started spreading malicious rumors about him. After a while, the man began to feel remorse for what he had done, and he went to the rabbi to ask forgiveness and to undertake any penance that the rabbi might impose upon him. The rabbi told him to take a feather pillow, cut it up, and let the wind scatter the feathers. The man did so and then returned to the rabbi.

"Am I now forgiven?" he asked.

"Almost. You have one more thing to do, and then you will be forgiven," said the rabbi.

"What's that?" asked the man.

"Go and gather up all the feathers you have dispersed, put them back in the pillow, and sew it up as it was before you cut it open. Then you will be forgiven."

"But that's not possible," said the man.

"Precisely," said the rabbi. "Though you want to repair the damage you have done, you cannot do so, just as you cannot gather up all the feathers and repair the pillow."

⊷ 10 ⊶

Your Money or Your Life

A man's treatment of money is the most decisive test of his character—how he makes it and how he spends it.

—JAMES MOFFATT, SCOTTISH BIBLICAL SCHOLAR

AND CHURCH HISTORIAN

*A*n May 1997, Chicago Bulls' coach Phil Jackson received an offer of $30 million to coach the Orlando Magic. The contract was for five years—$6 million per year, beginning with the 1997–1998 season. At the time, Jackson was well aware that if he did not accept the offer right away, it might be withdrawn, and that an equally lucrative offer might not be forthcoming in the future. It seemed to be an example of the axiomatic "offer you can't refuse." Nonetheless, Jackson announced that since the 1997 play-offs were then still in progress, he would not consider any offers until the play-offs were over.

Speaking to the press, Jackson said, "Money doesn't bring happiness. That's one of the things I think that people have to learn in life, that it doesn't bring happiness. If you learn that, you're better off for it."

If Phil Jackson is right that money doesn't guarantee happiness, then why do so many people value it so highly, work so hard to acquire it, and sacrifice so much to accumulate it? Because they think it does.

People tend to confuse money with things it is not—like happiness. Money may be a *symbol* of many things, like happiness, success, and security. But, in itself, money is none of those things. A symbol is never the same as what it symbolizes. Though money is probably coveted more than any other thing in the world, it has no intrinsic worth. Its value is vested in why and how it is used. Indeed, sometimes it can prove to be of no value at all. Consider the following two examples.

On the old television series *Gilligan's Island*, a group of people are stranded on a tropical island. Among them are the billionaires Thurston Howell III and his wife, Lovey. A chest full of money and jewels sits in their hut. But all of their money is useless on the island. Nothing can be bought with it. It cannot provide food, shelter, security, or happiness. It has no real value, no intrinsic worth. Real wealth on the island cannot be measured by how many dollars are in a chest, but by items and skills that can be used to enhance the quality of the lives of those stranded there.

My colleague, Brenda, has hypoglycemia, a form of diabetes. We were once attending a conference together when she had a diabetic attack caused by a sharp drop of her blood sugar. She needed something sweet immediately in order to recover. There was a candy machine near the conference room. It took change only, but I had no change. The lowest currency I had was a $20 bill. In itself, in that crisis, it was useless. I went from person to person, explaining the situation, begging for two quarters. When that didn't work, I offered to exchange the $20 bill for two quarters. People ignored me, thinking me crazy. Finally, a woman, herself a diabetic, came with me to Brenda's side and gave her some tablets that she always carried with her for her own condition. Brenda had been in danger of lapsing into diabetic shock, but my money was of no use. In that situation, a $20 bill was of no value. A check or a $100 bill would also have been of no value. Two quarters would have been worth much more.

The value of money is determined by what you can do with it in a particular situation. Both on Gilligan's Island as well as off of it, money has no value in itself. The value of money depends upon whether and how it can serve to enhance the quality of life. How we think about money often tells us a great deal about how we think about ourselves, about what we value. "Money talks"— but what does it say?

Ask people to make a single wish that they would like fulfilled, and many will tell you that it would be to be rich. But then ask them if they would prefer riches to happiness, and most would opt for happiness and fulfillment. Ask them whether they would prefer riches or good health and longevity, and most would relent on their wish for riches. From this we see that there are many things that people value more highly than money, that wealth is not synonymous with happiness. Why, then, do so many people dream about being rich?

If asked why they want to be rich, most people will tell you that having a lot of money would provide them with comfort, security, power, respect, and happiness. In other words, it's not really money that they want—it's what they believe money can acquire for them. Being rich is not an end in itself, but a means to an end, a vehicle rather than a destination.

For many people, however, acquiring riches can become an end in itself. The reasons why a person originally desired to amass financial wealth can readily be eclipsed by the obsession with acquiring more and more wealth. Though a person may tell you that health and family are more important than acquiring more wealth, his actions are the true test of whether he believes what he says. In the 1987 movie *Wall Street*, one of the characters, played by veteran actor Hal Holbrook, says, "The main thing about money: It makes you do things you don't want to do."

In history, legend, movies, and our daily newspapers, we hear about people caught up in the never-ending treadmill of acquiring more and more simply for the purpose of acquiring more and more. The nature of this addiction is described in the biblical book of Ecclesiastes: "A lover of money never has his fill of money, nor the lover of wealth his fill of income . . . the rich man's abundance does not let him sleep." The myth of King Midas and the Christmas story of Scrooge tell us that the acquisition of wealth simply for its own sake brings neither happiness nor fulfillment because it confuses ends with means, goals with the path toward reaching them. Certainly, it is a blessing to have money and the things that money can buy, but it is important, every once in a while, to make sure that we have not lost the things that money can't buy.

"Money can't buy me love," the Beatles sang. Nor can it buy other things we value most, like happiness. From Ecclesiastes to Phil Jackson, people have continuously discovered and rediscovered this simple truth. Nonetheless, throughout much of American history, we have been led to believe that happiness will be attained and increased as we acquire and consume more and more.

Ours is a consumer society where we are encouraged by advertisements to believe that the more we have, the more we are. This conviction is preached incessantly through every American television set, although it is denied by almost every religion and philosophy known to humankind. Built into the mentality of the consumer society is what has been called the premise of dissatisfaction: No matter how much we have, it is never enough. The hope implanted by advertising is that the next purchase will yield happiness, then the next, and the next. What do most Americans want? Look at advertisements. If you were an anthropologist a century from now reconstructing American society's deepest concerns and values on the basis of today's advertisements, you would be convinced that what Americans of our times were most concerned about were loose dentures, armpit odor, beer, and building up their abdominal muscles.

Oscar Wilde once wrote that there are two tragedies in life. One is *not* getting what we want. The other is getting what we want. Further, sometimes getting what we want or what we think we want turns out to be the greater of the two tragedies. Or, as an old proverb puts it, "Be careful what you pray for, because you might get it." Eventually, we may have to confront the daunting problems: After satisfaction, what? Now that I have it all, is this all that there is?

At restaurants, they used to ask if you "want" cream with your coffee. I have noticed that they now ask whether you "need" cream with your coffee. It's as if I might expire instantly if I don't get cream for my coffee. This change of language indicates a change in perspective. Wants and desires have become needs. The fulfillment of any need is almost considered a constitutional right. Needs have replaced values and visions as a basis for action. Needs have become ends in themselves rather than means to ends. But neither a person nor a society aimed solely at the satisfaction of perceived needs and desires will be able to survive for long. Needs as ends are dead ends. Once one is fulfilled, others appear to replace them. There is a fixed minimum of needs for all human beings, but no fixed maximum for any human being. Eventually, the bank runs out of capital, leaving us as dissatisfied as before.

We are living through a "needs epidemic" that threatens our spiritual health and well-being. Inauthentic needs created by fashion, advertisement, and envy threaten to smother our authentic and natural needs. Need easily turns into insatiable greed. When needs become ends in themselves, they can cause us to forfeit our freedom. We become imprisoned in a maze of insatiable, ever-expanding needs. Like rats who choose saccharine over a healthy diet and subsequently starve to death, we tend to starve our souls by feeding them junk food.

Money can offer us freedom. But how many carriers of the old "MasterCharge" credit card were either masters or in charge of their lives? The constant encouragement from society to produce and consume in a never-ending spiral can lead us to a form of indentured servitude where we must earn more to pay for goods and services of which we have no need. Ours is a consumer society where each of us is in spiritual danger of being consumed. The real question is, do we have money, or does money have us? As the eminent British statesman Edmund Burke said, "If we command our wealth, we shall be rich and free; if our wealth commands us, we are poor indeed." Why do we want to work "for nothing"? Why do we work harder and harder for what we don't really need while the costs to our moral and spiritual lives continue to mount? As we become obsessed by artificially induced desires, our deeper needs become eclipsed. Our proclivity for instant gratification threatens to undermine our quest for more durable sources of happiness and meaning.

In the 1960s, a psychologist conducted a remarkable experiment regarding instant gratification. He gave a group of four-year-olds the following choice: If you want a marshmallow, you can have one now. But if you want two marshmallows, you must wait a while until I return from running an errand, which will take 15 to 20 minutes. How each of the children responded was recorded—who took the single marshmallow immediately and who waited, thereby delaying immediate gratification. Many years later, the participants, now teenagers, were located. The emotional and social difference between those who grabbed the marshmallow and those who delayed gratification was dramatic. Those who resisted immediate gratification at four were now, as adolescents, more socially competent, personally effective, self-assured, and better able to cope with life's frustrations. They were also better able to deal with stress, less likely to be rattled by setbacks, and more likely to embrace, pursue, and succeed in challenges without giving up. They were more independent, self-reliant, and dependable. They were more likely to take initiative. More than a decade later, they were still able to delay gratification in pursuit of their goals. Some years later, the participants were tested again. Those who had waited were found to be more academically competent, articulate, reasonable, and eager to learn, and they were better able to make and to execute a plan. Their scores on the SAT exam were an average of 210 points higher than those who had immediately taken the single marshmallow at the age of four.

Though it contradicts the wisdom of experience and the teachings of most of the moral traditions of the world, the consumer society urges instant gratification rather than discipline and self-control, short-term fixes rather than enduring satisfaction. In this type of society, the unrestrained desire to "have it all" becomes one's motto. This is the message of Aesop's famous tale of "The Goose That Laid the Golden Egg."

A man and his wife had the good fortune to own a goose that laid a golden egg every day. Lucky though they were, they soon began to think that they were not getting rich fast enough, and thinking that the goose must be made of gold inside, they decided to kill it. But when they had killed it and cut it open, they discovered that it was just like any other goose. The moral of the story: Much wants more and loses all.

A contemporary version of Aesop's tale is the story of junk bond manipulators Ivan Boesky and Michael Milken, which was dramatized in the movie *Wall Street*. They had discovered "the goose that laid the golden egg" on Wall Street. But more was never enough. In 1985, Boesky delivered the commencement address at a prestigious business school in California. His message to the graduates about to enter the world of business and finance was that "greed is healthy," that it is a virtue. In the movie version, Michael Douglas gives a similar speech where he says, "Greed is good. Greed is right. Greed works. Greed clarifies. . . . Greed will save the United States." But the greed of Boesky, Milken, and others led to the collapse of banks and venerable Wall Street firms, to the Savings and Loan crisis of the 1980s, and to financial losses incurred by many people. Greed overtook all other considerations, including loyalty and commitment to one's colleagues, stewardship of others' money, and the public trust. Both Boesky and Milken were indicted and convicted. Each paid enormous fines, and each was imprisoned. There is a moral price for unbridled ruthlessness and greed. As Michael Douglas's character puts it in the film, "I was 'roasted' at a dinner, and someone said, 'Why are we honoring this man? Have we run out of human beings?'"

The acquisition and expenditure of money is like fire. Just as fire, when used responsibly, can warm us on a cold night or, when used irresponsibly, can destroy our home and possessions, money can bring us comfort or it can consume us. It depends upon how we think about it. Money is a tool that can either be used to harm or to elevate life. Wealth must be wed with wisdom. Money is neither good nor bad; it all depends upon how we use it.

Money is not synonymous with either wealth or success. Rather, it is a measurement of one kind of wealth and of one va-

riety of success. Wealth and success come in many forms—of
which financial success is only one. Indeed, there are forms of
wealth unrelated to money, such as the gift of friendship and the
bestowal of love. In the final analysis, wealth and success are not
measured by what we have, but by who we become. True wealth
and authentic success are characterized by the acquisition of
wisdom and the tranquillity of contentment.

While money is no guarantor of happiness, neither is the lack
of money. While some consider poverty to be a virtue, most experience it as a catastrophe. Poverty is a calamity because it en-
dangers life itself. The destitute person is threatened by malnu-
trition, the elements of nature—cold, heat, rain, and snow—and
by inadequate clothing and shelter. He is psychologically endangered by feelings of powerlessness, dependency, and of simply
being ignored by the more economically fortunate. Poverty can
readily lead to desperation, and desperate people do desperate
things. Deprivation may readily lead to depravity. Abject dependency can easily strip a person of the will to try to improve his
situation.

We can hardly expect a person who is concerned about the
source of his next meal, shelter for the night, or necessary ex-
penditures that cannot be paid to have the peace of mind required
for focusing on the cultivation of the moral virtues. As Aristotle
pointed out, and as psychologist Abraham Maslow has more recently affirmed, without a modicum of financial security, a person
becomes too distracted by his "creature needs" to attend to the
development of the spiritual, intellectual, and moral dimensions
of life. In our society, money is a necessity of life. As a medieval
rabbi put it, "The Hebrew word for money is *damim* which also
means 'blood' because just as blood sustains a person's life, so is
money essential for life." Or as the old adage puts it, "Rich or
poor, it's good to have money."

Many people think that if they had fiscal security, their
problems would dissolve and their moral temptations would
somehow disappear. But that is not the case. Because they have
more to lose, constant worry and moral temptation are per-

haps more prevalent among the rich than among the poor and middle class.

↤

"The more you have, the more afraid you are of losing it," a very wealthy widow once confided in me. We were in a taxicab on the way to her house for dinner. She instructed the driver to stop around the corner from her house.

"Why are we stopping here?" I asked.

"Because it costs another 50 cents if we wait for the light to change and for the taxi to turn the corner."

↤

As the character played by Darryl Hannah in *Wall Street* puts it, "Once you've had money and lost it, it's worse than not having had it at all."

Studies have consistently shown that being well-off does not corrolate to being well. Once beyond poverty, further economic growth does not make people appreciably happier. Studies in the United States during the post–World War II era showed a negligible correlation between a rising standard of living and how happy people considered themselves to be. Similarly, studies in various Western European countries found that a higher gross national product per capita did not necessarily indicate a higher degree of satisfaction with life.

Though many people believe that if they won the lottery, their problems would be solved and they would be happier, studies of lottery winners have consistently found something quite different. While lottery winners described themselves as exhilarated and extremely happy immediately after winning, that level of happiness quickly faded. Surveyed a year or more after winning, most considered themselves less happy than they were a year before winning. "How many hats can you buy for one head?" said one instant millionaire.

A startling comparative study was done by a group of social psychologists who measured how happy people felt themselves to be. The people were from three groups: winners of the Illinois State Lottery, a control group of random people, and victims of accidents that had left them paraplegics. The study revealed that the lottery winners were generally no happier than those in the control group. Additionally, the lottery winners found significantly less gratification in a series of mundane activities, such as eating a good meal or listening to music, than the victims of accidents.

What has been consistently found in study after study is that how much people have is not an accurate indicator of how happy they consider themselves to be. Rather, the size of the gap between what people have and what they want is consistently the most significant indicator of how happy people consider themselves to be. People who have what they want and who want what they have are generally the most happy. People whose wants substantially exceed what they have are the most dissatisfied and unhappy—no matter how much they might have. The wisdom of the Talmudic proverb rings true here: Who is wealthy? He who is happy with what he has.

Once I received a request to make a hospital visit to see a man who had been a student of mine. He had had a heart attack followed by triple bypass surgery. His name is Louis, and he is the chief executive officer and a major stockholder of a company listed on the Fortune 1000. His doctor was a friend of mine, and he was surprised that I knew Louis.

"I wouldn't want to do business with him," my friend warned me. "But when he found out that I was your friend, he asked me if I could persuade you to visit him."

Louis rarely participated in class discussion. Occasionally, he would ask a question. I was never sure why he attended my classes. As I entered his hospital room, I had a hunch that I was going to find out.

After we exchanged pleasantries, Louis said, "Thanks for coming. Undoubtedly, you're wondering why I asked you to come. Well, it's for the same reason that I took your classes. I need something more in my life than business. And lying here, it hit me even harder. I have a lot of money, influence, and power.

Yet when I awoke after my operation, barely able to move, grateful for simply being alive, I realized how transitory, how illusionary, it all is. I thought I was going to die, and sayings like 'shrouds have no pockets' and 'you can't take it with you' ran through my head. What's that saying of the Talmudic rabbis you cited in class about hands? I keep thinking about it."

"Do you mean the one that says: When a person is born, the hands are clenched, as though to say, 'All the world is mine, now I shall acquire it.' But when a person dies, the hands are wide open, as if to say, 'I have acquired nothing from the world.'"

"Yeah, that's the one. Lying here, I've realized more than ever that I need to get out of the rat race, because even if you win the rat race, you're still a rat."

"Did you ever read the biblical book of Ecclesiastes?" I asked.

"No, they must have skipped it in Sunday School," he said.

"Well, you remind me a little of Ecclesiastes," I said. "He was a rich and powerful man with deep inner fears and frustrations. He reached a point, probably during middle age, when he realized that wealth and power do not guarantee happiness and fulfillment, that he could get sick and die in pain and misery, and that wealth was not the answer to the problems that now preoccupied and perplexed him.

"Ecclesiastes had sampled all the pleasures and comforts of life that money could buy. He understood that time had become more precious and more limited than money and that reveling in wealth was really a way of escaping the challenge of discovering a dimension of meaning in his life. He was asking himself the most challenging questions of all: Now that I have everything I want, what will my life mean if it ends? Now that I have everything I desire, do I desire everything that I have? Why is having everything not enough? I am a man of means but not of meaning. What good is wealth if it cannot protect me against illness, death, and meaninglessness?

"Ecclesiastes is the great cynic of the Bible. Remember how Oscar Wilde describes a cynic—as a person who knows the price of everything but the value of nothing?"

There was a Bible in the hospital room, and I opened it and

read this passage from Ecclesiastes to Louis: "I amassed silver and gold. . . . I got enjoyment out of all my wealth, but that was all I got out of my wealth. . . . My thoughts turned to all the fortune my hands had built up, to the wealth I had acquired and won . . . and oh it was all futile and pursuit of wind; there was no real value under the sun. . . . And so I came to view with despair all the gains I had made under the sun."

"Bull's-eye," Louis said. "That's me to a tee."

"Have you ever heard of the Nobel Prize–winning philosopher Bertrand Russell?" I asked.

"No," said Louis, "but I think I am going to."

"Russell once wrote, 'When sound success comes, a man is already a nervous wreck, so accustomed to anxiety that he cannot shake off the habit of it when the need is past.' Does this sound familiar?"

"If I had heard that before, I wouldn't be here now," said Louis.

"If you can, read the book of Ecclesiastes. You will discover a lot about yourself there. But I want to remind you of something else someone once said."

"Another biblical guy or another philosopher?"

"Neither. Jack Benny.

"An armed robber comes up to Jack Benny, known for his stinginess, and says, 'Your money or your life.' Benny does not respond. The robber points the gun at him and demands again, 'Your money or your life.' Benny takes on a thoughtful pose. Getting agitated, the thief waves his gun and says, 'Didn't you hear me? Your money or your life.' To which Benny responds, 'I'm thinking about it.'

"Well, Louis, you're thinking about it, too, and what you are having trouble understanding is that it need not be either/or. You can have your money *and* your life. It depends on how you want to think about your money, how you want to think about your life, and what you want the relationship of the two to be. For sure, that relationship is not working now."

"So what should I do?" Louis asked.

"Look, Louis. Many people envy you—your wealth, your

power, your influence. Give me an example of someone *you* envy."

"There's a guy named Frank who works for me in our construction companies division. He's a crane operator. Last year, he won the lottery. $7 million. The day after winning, he came to see me. I thought that he was going to tell me off and quit. But he didn't. He came to ask me if he could keep his job and donate his salary to charity. I couldn't believe it. He told me he loved his job, he liked his co-workers, and he wouldn't know what to do with himself if he didn't work. I let him keep his job, and every month, we send his paycheck to a group of designated charities. I'm jealous of Frank because he loves what he's doing, he loves who he's doing it with, he's happy—with or without the millions. Maybe he's more secure with the money, but I have a lot more money than him, yet he's much happier than I am. So, sure, I'm jealous of him."

"Then perhaps you should try to be more like him. He has his money *and* his life. He's happy with who he is, with what he's doing, with who he's with. You've made many good investments throughout the years, and now you have a great deal to show for it. Maybe it's now time to 'give back' some of what you've acquired, and in so doing, to increase the value and the meaning of your own life. Consider yourself a portfolio of underdeveloped investments that it is now time to develop. You've invested in many enterprises. Now it's time to invest in your own self. You may be surprised by the dividends. I know that you've made a fortune investing in art. Maybe now it's time to invest in the most important work of art—your own life. Use what you have to become who you can yet be."

A few days passed, and a letter came from Louis. It said, "No museum would want the art work I'm now working on. But when I shave, I like what I see in the mirror much better than before."

A week later, a messenger arrived in my office bearing a gift from Louis. I opened the envelope and tickets to Louis's skybox at the United Center for a Chicago Bulls' game fell out along with a photocopy of an article from the *Chicago Sun-Times*. A quote in the article was highlighted in yellow. It was by Phil Jackson.

"Money doesn't bring happiness. That's one of the things I think that people have to learn in life, that it doesn't bring happiness. If you learn that, you're better off for it." Scribbled on the photocopy in Louis's handwriting was the comment, "If you see Phil at the game, tell him he's right. I wish I knew it sooner. Thanks. Louis."

⮎

A medieval sage was once asked, "Who is greater, the wise or the rich?" He replied, "The wise." He was then asked, "If the wise are greater than the rich, then why are there more wise people at the doors of the rich than there are rich people at the doors of the wise?" He replied, "Because the wise appreciate the value of the riches while many of the rich do not similarly appreciate the value of wisdom."

11

The Gift of Friendship

No one would choose to live without friends,
even if he had all other goods.

—ARISTOTLE

Centuries ago, in the Holy Land, there lived a holy man whose name was Honi. One day while walking on the road, Honi noticed an old man planting a carob tree. Honi said to the man, "You know, it takes 70 years until a carob tree bears fruit. Why then do you plant a tree when you will not live long enough to eat of its fruit?"

"I found this world provided with carob trees when I came into it," said the man. "As my ancestors planted for me so that I might enjoy the fruit of what they planted, so I now plant, so that those who come after me might enjoy the fruit of what I have planted."

Honi went into a cave near where the old man was planting in order to reflect upon the wisdom of what the old man had told him. But as it happened, Honi fell into a deep sleep. He slept for 70 years, and when he awoke, he felt very refreshed, as if he had slept for many hours rather than for many years. As he left the cave, he saw large carob trees growing nearby. A man was gathering carobs from the trees and was eating them.

"Do you know who planted these trees?" Honi asked the man.

"My grandfather," the man replied.

"Then I must have slept for 70 years!" said the astonished Honi to the equally surprised man.

Honi then went to his house. A young man, whom he did not recognize, opened the door. Honi asked about the Honi who had lived in the house years before.

"He mysteriously disappeared years ago," said the young man.

"And where is the son of Honi?" Honi asked.

"After waiting many years for his father to return," said the young man, "the son of Honi sold this house to my father. But now, both my father and the son of Honi have died. However, Honi's grandson still lives in the town, and I will tell you how to get to his house."

Saddened by the news of the death of his son, and in shock that 70 years of his life had slipped into oblivion, Honi was enthused about meeting his grandson.

Honi went to the home of his grandson. He immediately recognized his grandson because he looked a lot like Honi's own father. He saw that his grandson had children of his own.

"Who are you, old man?" his grandson asked.

"I am Honi, your grandfather," Honi said. "I have been asleep for 70 years, but now I have returned."

Honi's grandson did not believe him, and he chased him away.

Honi then went to search for his friends, but all of them had died. When someone asked him who he was, he would say, "I am Honi," but no one believed him. Everyone he encountered knew of Honi's piety and his learning. Everyone knew the story of Honi's mysterious disappearance, around which many legendary embellishments had developed. But no one knew Honi. And so, despite the fame of his legacy, Honi was deeply grieved. All of those who had given his life meaning and significance had died. He was completely alone, without a friend in the world.

Honi returned to the cave in which he had slept for 70 years, and he prayed to God that he might die. Then he died. When this became known, a proverb was coined: "Either friendship or death." Without companionship, without friendship, life could hardly be worth living.

Whenever I think about the story of Honi, Jerry comes to mind. Jerry had made a fortune on the Chicago futures exchange, where things are sold and bought that do not yet exist. He and I served together on the board of a local charity. I had met Jerry a few times at board meetings, where we had exchanged amenities. He always begins a conversation by discussing the weather, then sports. He does so with great fervor and with authority in his convictions. He always seems enthused, effervescent, and perpetually happy. He seems to know and to be liked by everyone. He is the epitome of an American success story.

The son of immigrant parents, Jerry quit high school to go to work to help support his family. By 21, he was a millionaire. He has a beautiful wife, three healthy children, and a gigantic home in the suburbs. He owns a number of companies. He drives an antique sports car. Usually, he dresses in a flannel shirt and jeans, even at his office. I doubt whether he owns a tie. He is involved in many civic organizations and has the reputation of being "well-connected." But at the extravagant 40th birthday party that his wife threw for him at a lavish banquet hall, I saw another, unexpected side of Jerry.

The invitation to the party said, "Join Jerry and 300 of his friends to celebrate the big four-oh." I stopped by the party to pay my respects, expecting to leave after a short visit. But when Jerry saw me come in, he asked if he could talk to me privately. He ushered me into a small room. Next door, there was music, dancing, singing, and laughter. Mountains of food were being served and quickly consumed. There were thousands of balloons, clowns walking on stilts, fire-eaters, and magicians. Jerry closed the door, sat down, put his head in his hands, and began to cry. In a few seconds, he regained his composure, and he said, "I hardly know you, and here I am crying like a little kid in front of you. But I have a problem."

"What is it?" I asked.

"I'm 40," he said, and as he began to cry again, he blurted out, "and I have no friends. I just needed to tell someone, and it might as well be you."

"Have you ever read *Treasure Island*?"

"No, but I saw the movie with Robert Newton. But what has that got to do with my problem?"

"*Treasure Island* was written by Robert Louis Stevenson, and it was he who wrote, 'A friend is a gift you give yourself.' It seems that cultivating a friendship with someone is the best birthday present you could give to yourself."

"Thanks," Jerry said. "I guess I'll rejoin my party to see if there are any potential birthday presents for me out there."

Many of us recognize Jerry; he's the kind of person that we meet every day in our lives, in literature, and in proverbs. His tragedy is like that of Gatsby in *The Great Gatsby* by F. Scott Fitzgerald. Gatsby's life, like Jerry's, was filled with parties that were "enthusiastic meetings between people who never knew each other's names." He is like Willy Loman in Arthur Miller's tragic drama *Death of a Salesman*, who was "best liked," but who never knew who he was; surrounded by people, he was desperately and painfully lonely. Jerry's situation demonstrated the truth of the old proverb, "It's not good to be alone—even in paradise."

While Jerry's problem was not an enviable one, he was better off than he thought. Many people in his situation fail to recognize either the cause of, or the solution to, their malaise. At least he understood what his problem was, and he knew the remedy for it. Jerry realized that cultivating friendship can serve as an antidote to the anxiety, depression, emptiness, and listlessness that being friendless and lonely can bring.

Rather than seeking the elixir of friendship, some people try to delude themselves into believing that they are not *really* alone and friendless. Some use frenzied activity as a substitute for confronting their forlorn selves. This exercise in self-deception is based on the view that we are only really alive when we are *doing* something. But always being in a hurry can be a camouflage for anxiety, loneliness, and insecurity, a pseudo-demonstration of one's false sense of self-importance.

Some people seem prepared to endure a variety of indignities in order to deceive themselves into believing that they're not really alone. They will allocate substantial resources of time and money to mind-numbing activities or initiate an unwanted string of unsatisfying sexual liaisons in order to fill a personal void. Or they'll submit themselves to hours of vacuous television or assault their ears with incessantly loud music to dispel the silence and loneliness they would otherwise have to confront.

"One of the reasons I have a problem making friends," Jerry told me when we next met, "is because I've been burned so many times. I have a lot of influence and money, so people often pretend that they're my friends in order to get something from me. Do they think I'm so stupid? Don't they realize that I can see behind their phony smiles, that I know a huckster when I see one? In my business, I have to read people accurately and often quickly. When a lot of money is at stake in a deal, I have to know who is for real and who is full of it. I may not know who my friends are, but, for sure, I know who they're not."

"What's the first signal you get from somebody that you can't trust them?" I asked Jerry.

"Trust is a feature of real friendship. I know that," Jerry said. "Maybe I've become too jaded to trust anyone anymore, and that's why I have no friends. The first signal is when someone I hardly know starts to flatter me. That's the tip-off. I know it's just a manipulative device to try to get something from me or to get me to do something for them. Do people really think I'm so gullible? I guess they do. I've read about how people need 'validation' from someone else to feel good about themselves, but as far as I'm concerned, it's a big con game. I've been to those motivational seminars where they tell you about the importance of 'communication' and 'relationship building.' But that's a big con game, too. All it does is teach people how to con each other. So now in business meetings, everybody has been to these seminars, and everybody is using the same techniques that they learned there to con one another the same way. But what seems to be lost in all this 'communication' is something really worth communicating. It's all touchy-feely nonsense. Sure, I've learned 'relationship building' in terms of how to cultivate and develop clients and customers, but not friends, not real relationships."

I asked Jerry if he knew the story of the Velveteen Rabbit.

"Sure," said Jerry. "Everyone who has kids knows that one."

I suggested to him that the Velveteen Rabbit is an example of a real friend, the opposite of a "fair-weather friend." Sometimes what we go through for a friend makes us a little worn and torn, like the Velveteen Rabbit, but that's what shows that the friendship is real. Like loyalty and courage, true friendship often shows itself most clearly when we are operating under stress.

"Since you reminded me of my kids, let me tell you that I may have done a lousy job choosing my own friends, but I sure as heck watch out for what kind of friends my kids have," Jerry said. "I want my kids to associate with good and decent kids. Not with brats. Not with smart alecks. Not with weirdos or juvenile delinquents."

"Why is that?" I asked Jerry.

"Because," he said, "what kinds of friends kids have rubs off on them."

Jerry had just summarized an important insight of the ancient Greek philosopher Plato on the nature of friendship. Plato taught that we can learn a great deal about a person's character from the friendships that person seeks and sustains. Who a person chooses for his friends tells us a great deal about that person. Like all of the moral virtues, friendship indicates who and what we value, who and what matters most to us. Our friendships are a reflection of who we are as well as a catalyst for crafting who we can yet become.

Our sporadic meetings took place over a number of months, usually whenever Jerry felt the need to talk. Each time we met, it became progressively clear to me that he had an increasingly good grasp on what he was looking for. Each time we met, I gave him some "homework," something short to read, written by a variety of thinkers, mostly philosophers, on the nature of friendship. Yet the clearer it became to Jerry as to what friendship entailed, the more he began to back away from it. He liked the idea of friendship and cherished the value of it, but he seemed unable and unwilling to take the leap of commitment that the cultivation of friends requires.

Like many businessmen I have known, Jerry was more willing to take risks in his professional and business life than in his personal life. He was willing to risk large sums of money on a hunch, but he didn't seem prepared to risk intimacy with another person, perhaps for fear of being hurt later on, for fear of not being a winner. While he willingly made full financial disclosure to his lawyer and to his accountant, Jerry doubted whether he could make full personal disclosure to a friend. While he confided in his psychotherapist, Jerry remained reluctant to open himself up to a friend. As Jerry put it to me, "I can sue the pants off my shrink, but I couldn't sue a friend for revealing my secrets."

Authentic friendship entails the intimacy of mutual disclosure, but Jerry did not appear willing enough to risk the vulnerability that comes with self-disclosure. Nor was he patient or caring enough to listen to the disclosures of others. To be sure, he had little tolerance for the phony compliments paid him by others. Yet he habitually complimented everyone with whom he spoke, including me. Each time we met, Jerry would begin our conversation with a shower of accolades about me. He always became overly defensive when criticized, and I wondered whether he could take constructive criticism, even from a true friend. It never seemed to occur to him that a true friend is not one who simply reaffirms our public persona, who always approves of our actions, but that an authentic friend is someone who is willing to take the risk of being completely candid. A real friend is not one who always tells us what we want to hear, but someone who we can count on to tell us what we sometimes need to hear for our own good.

I told Jerry about a group of Hasidic Jews who lived in nineteenth-century Poland. They practiced an unusual custom regarding friendship called the "communion of friends." At least once a week, and more if they needed it, a person would go with his best friend to a secluded place for a few hours, and there he would talk about his most secret feelings, exhilarating joys, heart-wrenching disappointments, fervent hopes, deepest fears, highest aspirations, noblest achievements, devastating failures, and wildest fantasies. Then, at another time during the week, the friend would do the same. Again, Jerry liked the idea, but when I asked him whether he could see himself doing it, he recoiled as if he were having an allergic reaction.

Jerry did his homework. As we talked, he peppered his conversation with quotes he remembered from the material I had given him to read. He cited William Blake, who said, "The bird a nest, the spider a web, man friendship." He often quoted Plato's statement, "I have a passion for friends, and I would rather have a good friend than all the possessions in the world." Jerry had the passion of which Plato spoke, but he didn't have the will to translate it into action.

I was reminded of the old story about the person who was in love with the idea of love but who couldn't establish a love-relationship with another person. While Jerry was unusually effective in cultivating his long-time clients, he did not seem prepared to make a long-term investment in developing friendships. When he spoke of the friends he hoped to make, his focus always was on what they could do for him, how they could fill his needs, but never on fundamental characteristics of friendship that seemed to elude him, such as empathy, intimacy, and reciprocity.

Jerry just could not get it through his head that *having* a friend entails *being* a friend, being there for a friend, *befriending* someone else. Jerry, who was so used to doing cost-benefit analyses in his business life, knew no other way of evaluating a relationship, even in his private life. For Jerry, everything was a trade-off, even in his relationship with his wife. He could not assimilate the idea that once a friendship becomes subject to an audit, once a balance sheet determines the value and the perpetuation of a friendship, it is not likely to be a very durable relationship.

The British writer Boswell wrote about the need "to keep friends in repair." By this, he was referring to the constant care and tenderness that developing, cultivating, and maintaining friendships requires. Jerry couldn't buy into this attitude. He said that he wanted love and friendship, but what he really meant was that he wanted people to love and to befriend *him*. Unlike the Velveteen Rabbit, becoming a little worn and torn in the service of others was not part of Jerry's game plan. To use his expression, that wasn't "a win-win situation."

In his groundbreaking book *Future Shock*, Alvin Toffler noted that our society has not only created a culture of disposable items but also of disposable people. Ours is a culture of transitory relationships where people come together in an implicit "give and get" contract, but as soon as the relationship is no longer "functional," it ends. Here, one cannot expect abiding friendships, but only the convergence of transitory needs, where people—as novelist John Barth puts it—"float past." This attitude has replaced earlier classical views that describe friendship as embracing components such as commitment, constancy, communion, compassion, empathy, reciprocity, loyalty, honesty, tenderness, openness, character-building, and love. These classical views understand friendship as something measured in decades of close association rather than something determined by passing fancies and ephemeral needs.

Jerry did his homework, but he couldn't pass the final exam. When asked if he would come to the aid of his friend unconditionally, Jerry couldn't say yes. He could readily imagine dropping everything to close a deal, but he couldn't conceive of setting things aside to come to the help of a friend. When asked whether he was willing to risk the intimacy and communion that friendship entails, he couldn't say yes. For Jerry, the decisive question is always, "What's in it for me, now?" Both in his business and his personal life, Jerry wanted only short-term investments, with minimal calculable risks, that "paid off big time." He bought himself many gifts for his 40th birthday, but the one gift that only he could acquire for himself—the gift of friendship—was just too expensive for him.

A few months passed until I saw Jerry again. We met by chance at a restaurant. He seemed unusually cheerful. He asked me to step into the men's room so that we could talk privately. Luckily, it was empty.

"Jerry, you look terrific," I said. "I have a feeling you've found a friend."

"No," said Jerry, "I've found something even better—a hobby."

"What hobby?" I asked.

"Skydiving," said Jerry.

I have a feeling that if I'm present at Jerry's 50th birthday, I'm going to find him in a little room, crying, with his head in his hands, saying, "Now I'm 50, and I have no friends." Jerry took up skydiving instead of friendship for many reasons, but the main reason was that he was ready to accept but not to give love.

Friendship is a form of love called *philia* by the ancient Greeks. Without friendship, love is a facade. Without love, friendship is like a body without a soul. Like all the moral virtues, loving friendship indicates who and what we value, who and what matters most to us. And, like all the moral virtues, friendship is a critical building block in the creation of a life of meaning and value, in the creation of life as a work of art. The ancient Roman philosopher Seneca said, "Of all felicities, the most charming is that of a firm and gentle friendship. It sweetens our cares, dispels our sorrows, and counsels us in all extremities."

↭

A faithful friend is a strong protection;
One who has found a friend has found a true treasure.
A faithful friend is beyond price,
And his value cannot be weighed.
A faithful friend is a life-giving medicine.

—THE WISDOM OF SIRACH

12

Crazy about Your Kids

Children are a gift of God,
Fruit of the womb God's reward.

—Psalm 127:3

A man had an only child, a son. The son was already an adult when his father died. The father left a will bequeathing everything he owned to his son. But there was an unusual clause in the will. The clause read, "My only son will inherit everything I have, but only when he starts acting foolishly."

This case actually came before a rabbinical court in Israel during the second century. The rabbis who served as judges on this court could not resolve the case. For days, they discussed this unusual clause, trying to figure out its meaning. Finally, not knowing how to decide the case, they went to seek the advice of one of the great rabbis of those days. His name was Joshua ben Korha.

When they arrived at the home of this great sage, they found him playing "horsie" with his young son. The famous scholar was crawling on his hands and knees, neighing like a horse. His young son was on his back laughing and screaming, "Giddy-up horsie!" Not wanting to disturb him, the rabbis left his house.

143

The next day, when Rabbi Joshua ben Korha came to the academy, the other rabbis asked his opinion on the difficult case before them.

Rabbi Joshua began to laugh, and he said to his colleagues, "You should already know the answer. Did you not visit my house yesterday? Did you not see how I was playing 'horsie' with my son? Did I not look foolish pretending to be a horse? The statement in the will simply means that the man's son will inherit everything when the son becomes a father, for when a person has children, it is not unusual to act foolishly and irrationally when it comes to them."

Plato described love as a form of madness. Certainly, the love of a parent for a child may appear to others as a form of foolishness or a manifestation of irrationality—although it is often a form of unabashed love. But the case that came before Joshua ben Korha anticipated the insight of the Yiddish expression, "Meshuggah fun kinder," which may have two meanings: A person is crazy when it comes to his children, or children make their parents crazy. Indeed, both may be true. It's like the old saying, "Insanity runs in my family. I inherited it from my children."

For many of us, the most important part of creating a legacy of goodness is when we become parents. Yet it's likely that most of us wouldn't be hired as qualified applicants for this job if we had to apply for it. Just being crazy about our children or crazy because of our children is not enough to make a person a good parent. Even if someone is an experienced parent, that is not enough to make that person a good and effective parent.

Surprisingly, when we look at the Bible, we find that most of the great biblical personalities—whether they were experienced parents or not, whether they were crazy about their children or not—were not successful at being parents. Indeed, it is surprising that the great figures of the Bible were great in many ways, but not as parents. For example, the first parents, Adam and Eve, raised two boys in a loving environment, but look at what one did to the other. Cain killed Abel. Moses is remembered for his greatness as a liberator, prophet, leader, and lawgiver, but not as an effective or successful father. The biblical role models we revere for so many things were, for the most part, failures as parents. You do not have to read further than the Book of Genesis to find families plagued by alcoholism, fratricide, incest, physical and verbal abuse, and deception. The great figures of the Bible can teach us many things, but they can't teach us the best way to parent.

The Bible tells the story of Isaac and his family. He and his wife Rebecca have two sons, Esau and Jacob, who are fraternal twins. Isaac is already elderly, and his eyesight has weakened. Isaac, a docile person from a wealthy family, was the son of Abraham. He favors his son Esau, the firstborn, who is everything Isaac never was: tall, strong, athletic—an outdoors type. Rebecca dotes on her younger son, Jacob, a homebody, for whom she wants a secure and successful future. She deals with her own frustrations by living vicariously through Jacob. Rebecca wants Jacob to become someone she couldn't and to accomplish things she didn't, and these ambitions know neither bounds nor scruples.

Rebecca eavesdrops as Isaac tells Esau to hunt down some game and prepare his favorite dish from it. She hatches a plot to further her ambitions for Jacob. Rebecca has Jacob get some animals from their flock. She prepares their meat into Isaac's favorite dish. She then dresses Jacob up to look and to smell like Esau and sends him to his father with the meal. Isaac, whose sight is dim, falls for the ruse. He gives Jacob the inheritance and the blessing meant for Esau.

When Esau arrives later that day, having done what his father asked him to do, Isaac informs him that the blessing and the inheritance meant for him have already been given to his brother. Despite the fraud committed against him and Esau by his wife and Jacob, Isaac lets his decision stand. Predictably, Esau gets angry. Rebecca realizes what she has done. She has alienated herself from Isaac and Esau. She has alienated her two sons from one another. Afraid that the powerful Esau will kill Jacob in anger, she sends Jacob away to her brother in a distant town. Rebecca is left with both a husband who doesn't trust her and a son whose affection she has betrayed.

From that time onward, Jacob leads a life of continued tragedy. He is deceived by his uncle and then by his wife, Leah.

His beloved wife Rachel dies in childbirth, and later he is tricked by his children. Like his parents, he plays favorites with his children, and he places his son Joseph above all others. Joseph's brothers become jealous of him, sell him as a slave, and tell Jacob that Joseph is dead. Toward the end of his life, Jacob sadly sums up his existence by saying, "The years of my sojourn on the earth have been few and hard."

Isaac and Rebecca failed as parents because they didn't fulfill the primary and essential part of the job description of parenting, and that is pedagogy. The primary feature of parenting is teaching ideals, traditions, and moral values that will help make the child a responsible adult. A parent *must* serve as a moral role model.

The Bible commands children to honor and obey their parents, but before expecting honor and respect, the parent must first ask, "What is it about me that deserves and that could evoke honor, respect, and love from my child?" This is precisely where Rebecca and Isaac failed. Rather than drawing their children away from falsehood, Rebecca and Isaac gave them no choice but to enter into it. Moral values are not imparted genetically. They are taught by example. Children need to be shown how to incorporate kindness into their character, how to make virtue a habit.

The Bible tells us that Isaac was blind, and some of the biblical commentators say that he was not only bereft of sight but also that he was bereft of awareness of and responsibility for his own family. He did not teach his sons what they needed to know in order to make their way in the world. He did not show them the way to mold their moral character, to create their lives as works of art. Distrust rather than trust, hate rather than love, alienation rather than solidarity was created between father and son, mother and son, and brother and brother. Isaac and Rebecca demonstrate how an error in judgment can have a profound and disasterous effect on not just one generation of children, but on several.

According to the Bible, Isaac favored Esau because he was a man of action, a hunter. Perhaps Isaac, who is described by the Bible as a very passive figure, saw in Esau the man he himself had always wished to be—active, virile, a sportsman. Perhaps Isaac favored Esau because Isaac wanted to live vicariously through him. And perhaps Isaac did not favor the more gentle, more passive Jacob because in him he saw too much of a reflection of his own self.

We are not told by the biblical text why Rebecca favored Jacob. But it may be that she favored Jacob over Esau not because of who Jacob was, but simply because she found it difficult to tolerate Esau's brusque and rough-edged nature, which she might have found offensive to her own tender sensibilities.

Rather than allowing their children to grow according to their own unique natures and to develop their individual talents, Isaac and Rebecca tried to shape their children in the image of their own needs to overcome their own frustrations. The real tragedy of the story, however, is that Jacob made the same mistakes in raising his children that his parents made in raising him—and he made a few even worse mistakes all on his own. Consequently, Isaac and Rebecca's mistakes continued to have an impact on the lives of their grandchildren. Yet a happy part of the story is the reconciliation of Esau and Jacob. Because each developed into adulthood in his own unique and particular way, the two siblings could eventually approach one another as friends, as brothers, and as independent adults.

❧

As each child moves toward maturity, he is confronted with the challenge of developing his innate talents and abilities in order to create his life as a work of art. The job of the parent is to act as a guide, as a rudder, to direct the child as he embarks on this life-long task. Poised to forge a unique path in the world, each child needs the wisdom, care, love, and guidance that only a parent can provide. Teachers and mentors can also play a significant role in this process, but they can never replace the parent.

Parents must summon all the wisdom they've accumulated to help them find a balance between nurture and discipline. A mother and father's hopes and expectations for their progeny can be optimistic, but they must also include a candid, realistic acknowledgment of their children's limitations. For example, a clumsy child may never become a gymnast; a child without musical talent won't play Mozart at Carnegie Hall. Parents must realize who their children are in order to help guide them toward what they can realistically become successful at.

A popular expression is that parents need to give their children roots and wings. Effective parenting aims at striking a balance between grounding the child in inherited traditions and values and encouraging the child to be independent, to think for himself.

Roots offer an anchor for personal identity and for moral integrity in an often rootless and sometimes ruthless society. Roots provide a foundation for meaning, a directional signal on the path of life.

In the early nineteenth century, the English radical John Thelwall once suggested to writer Samuel Taylor Coleridge that it is unfair for parents "to influence a child's mind by inculcating any opinions before it should have come to years of discretion and be able to choose for itself." When Thelwall came to visit Coleridge's home, Coleridge showed his guest the garden next to his house.

"But it is covered with weeds," said Coleridge's guest.

To which Coleridge replied, "That is only because the garden has not yet come to its age of discretion and choice. The weeds, you see, have taken the liberty to grow, and I thought it unfair of me to prejudice the soil towards roses and strawberries." A child, especially a young child, is like a garden that needs constant tending. The parent is a gardener who tends this garden.

By habituating a child to the practice of moral virtue, the parent not only fulfills a duty to the child but also to society—past, present, and future. By rooting the child in the moral wisdom of the past, a continuous link is forged in the chain of tradition. In later life, the child becomes enabled to apply the wisdom of the past to contemporary perplexities. The hard-won insights of past experience become a precious legacy bequeathed and transmitted from the past to the future. The child is provided with a foundation, an inspiration, a direction, for independent moral decision making in later life. What the great baseball player

Babe Ruth wrote toward the end of his life about religious teachings also holds true of moral teachings: "As far as most kids go, once religion sinks in, it stays there—deep down. The lads who get religious training get it where it counts—*in the roots.* They may fail it, but it never fails them. When the score is against them, or they may get a bum pitch, that unfailing Something inside will be there to draw on."

Since ancient times, philosophers have depicted the family as the foundation of society. When the family functions well, the larger society can function better. When the family serves as a conduit for moral values, the larger society is strengthened. The very stability and continuity of a society and of a culture depends, in the view of these philosophers, on how well the family conveys the insights and values of the past to the future.

Once there was a saintly man who tried to instill in his son the moral virtues. One day, they were walking together down the main street of the town in which they lived. Suddenly, they came upon the town drunkard and his son, both of whom were, of course, drunk. They stumbled along for a while, and eventually they sat down to rest in the gutter. "I envy that man," said the saintly man to his son about the town drunkard. "He has accomplished the goal of teaching his son to live according to his values. I only hope that he is not more successful with his son than I will be with you." The parent who offers either wings without roots or roots without wings will one day regret it.

Just as raising a child is usually more complicated than conceiving one, so cutting the umbilical cord when the child is grown up is more painful than cutting it when the child is first born. Yet the supreme goal in parenting is for the parent to nurture the child's abilities so that the child can become independent of the parent. Perpetuating parental dependency is not a hallmark of effective parenting. Preparing the child to make his own way in the world is.

According to the Talmudic rabbis, a parent is obliged to teach his child not only moral values but other things as well, such as how to be a good and productive citizen. The parent is further obliged to be sure that the child has the means to be economically independent by ensuring that the child receives education and training in a profession or craft. According to the Talmud, a parent who neglects this duty is as if he taught a child how to steal, because an economically dependent child would be obliged to rely on others for his own sustenance. One Talmudic tradition even requires the parent to be sure the child knows how to swim. Why? "Because his life may depend upon it." In other words, parents who have not taught their child "survival skills" as well as moral virtues have failed to fulfill their parental duty; they have fallen short of the job description of the effective parent.

In parenting, as in so many relationships that characterize our lives, balance is important: balance between roots and wings, between discipline and compassion. Discipline untempered by compassion can easily lead to child abuse, physical or verbal. Compassion unrestrained by discipline can encourage the child to become a moral anarchist. The undisciplined child often interprets the parent's behavior not as compassion, but as neglect. On the other hand, relentless and harsh discipline can backfire, stimulating the child to moral rebellion rather than to the instilling of moral habits. In the art of parenting, one must know when to be gentle and when to be firm, when to be insistent and when to be flexible, when to be compassionate and when to exercise parental authority. All the while, the primary task of parenting must be kept in mind: the moral development of the child.

Even the parent who excels in the moral part of parenting, even the parent who bestows complete and unconditional love upon his child, cannot expect that the child will always reciprocate such love. The parent's intense love for the child may abide, but the child will partially displace his love of the parent with the love of a significant other—with the love of a spouse, and especially with the love of his own child. As a Talmudic proverb states: "A parent's love is for his or her child, and that child's love is for his or her own children." Yet even when a child reaches adulthood, even when a child becomes a parent, the bonds of obligation and love toward his own parent endure—for though not everyone becomes the parent of a child, everyone is nonetheless the child of a parent. Both how we parent and how we treat our parents is part of the moral legacy we bestow on our children.

↢

Once there was an old man who lived with his son and his son's family. He had a pleasant life there, and he especially liked watching his young grandson grow from infancy to boyhood. But, as the years went on, his health began to fail. His hands shook, and often he would spill his food or drop a cup. Once his spoon hit his soup bowl by accident and spilled his soup all over the kitchen table. The bowl fell on the floor and shattered. This angered his son, who shouted at him, "If you can't eat with us, maybe you should eat or even live elsewhere. I'm tired of your sloppy habits. I'm tired of you breaking all of our good dishes."

The following day, the son gave his father a wooden bowl and a wooden spoon, and from that day on the old man stayed in his room most of the time and ate his meals there all alone. All of this caused him great pain.

One day, the son came home from work and his son gave him some things he had made in school: a wooden spoon and a wooden bowl.

"Are these for me?" the son asked.

"Yes," said his son. "When you are old and sick like Grandpa, and you come to live with me, you'll be able to use them when you eat alone in the room I'll give you to live in."

The son then ran to his father's room, asked his forgiveness, and invited him to rejoin the family at dinner.

↢

The "baby boom" generation also has been called the sandwich generation because many of its members are sandwiched in between taking care of their children during an often prolonged period when their children are getting an education to enter and become established in professions, and taking care of their parents as they become increasingly aged and often also progressively infirm. Parental care, especially of infirm and very aged parents, can stretch the limits of filial love and responsibility. It can be both a financial and psychological drain, especially if a person is helping to support his parents while also helping to support his children as they begin to establish themselves in new marriages, in new jobs, with new children of their own.

Sometimes role reversal occurs, where the child becomes like the parent, supporting the parent who once supported him. For example, a children's book called *Love You Forever* tells of a mother and her son, whom she rocks to sleep with the words, "I'll love you forever, I'll like you for always; as long as I'm living, my baby you'll be." Through the book, the boy grows up, and sometimes even as an adult, the mother rocks him to sleep. But in the last scene, the mother is too old and sick, and so the son holds his mother and gently rocks her to sleep with the same words.

There can come a time, however, when the psychological strain placed on adult children attempting to fulfill their filial duty may become too much to handle, especially if the parent becomes senile. In such a case, while the child is not freed from filial responsibility, professional help for the parent might be indicated. When this occurs, guilt must not stand in the way of acquiring professional assistance. The adult children cannot be expected to endanger their own health, to become fiscally destitute, and to neglect their own family in order to fulfill their responsibilities to a parent. Though responsibility remains, as in many other things, there must be balance.

In the Middle Ages, a type of will called an ethical will was often written by a parent for a child. This document dealt with moral values and lessons learned over a lifetime in a way that would benefit the recipient. What a beautiful tradition to bring back. It would be a way for parents to offer their children a summary of their deepest concerns. It provides an opportunity to say many things that ought to be said but that somehow are difficult to articulate in conversation. Writing an ethical will can be an important part of the art of parenting, and it is an exceptional way to practice being good.

Here are some topics that you might want to address in an ethical will.

- The world from which you came
- The formative events in your life
- The worst mistakes you made
- What you learned from those mistakes
- The people who influenced you most
- Your favorite possessions, and why you value them
- Your greatest achievements
- The dreams you fulfilled
- The dreams you left unfulfilled
- How you felt when . . . (for example, when your child was born)
- The day(s) you would like to relive
- What has been left unsaid that you would like to say
- Of whom you would like to ask forgiveness and who you would like to forgive
- What has been left undone that you would like to do
- What you want the reader to know from what you have learned from life
- Favorite sayings and proverbs
- The meaning of four-letter words like "love," "help," "care," "feel," and "give"

❧ 13 ❧

The World of Work

*Work by its very nature (is) about violence—to the spirit as well
as to the body. . . . It is, above all (or beneath all), about daily
humiliations. To survive the day is triumph enough for the
walking wounded. . . . It is about a search, too, for daily
meaning as well as daily bread, for recognition as well as cash,
for astonishment rather than torpor; in short, for a sort of life
rather than a Monday through Friday dying. Perhaps
immortality, too, is part of the quest—to be remembered. . . .*

—STUDS TERKEL, FROM *WORKING*

Suddenly, I was a manager, a boss, senior staff, administration. What do I do? How do I do it?

After serving as a professor for 13 years, teaching subjects like medieval philosophy and mysticism and writing scholarly books and articles on recondite subjects, I found myself vice president of a nonprofit educational institution. Rather than poring over medieval manuscripts, I now spent my time trying to decipher budgets and spreadsheets. Rather than reporting what the medievals had to say about a problem in metaphysics, I had scores of staff and faculty reporting to me about a myriad of administrative details. No longer was I immersed in the timeless world of ideas, but in the frenetic rush of a never-ending stream of apparently arbitrary deadlines and unrelated details.

Programs had to be designed and implemented. Policies and procedures had to be decided upon and then enforced. Reports had to be written and read. Piles of correspondence had to be answered. People paraded in and out of my office constantly. The telephone continuously rang. Faxes, e-mail, memos, messages, requests, and complaints filled up my "in-box" only moments after it had been emptied. Why did I subject myself to this? Why did I leave my "ivory tower" for the pressured rumble-tumble of management and administration? Could I manage a large staff? Could I manage myself in the midst of the daily challenge to make order out of chaos? When my son grew out of diapers, I was relieved that I would no longer have to clean up another person's mess. But, as a manager, I discovered that much of what I found myself doing was cleaning up other people's messes.

What is management all about, anyway? What is a manager, an executive, supposed to do? I had taken courses in graduate school in areas as far removed from management as could be imagined. Maybe I should take a course in management? I began to read textbooks on management. Like a student being introduced to a foreign language, I began to learn the vocabulary of management. It became increasingly clear to me that management is really organized common sense, but that it is a method with its own distinct vocabulary. By learning this vocabulary, I no longer felt like a stranger in a foreign country when CPAs and MBAs talked about administrative issues.

My apprehensions began to dissipate. Suddenly, things were beginning to fall into place. I had a new office, bigger and more comfortable than the one I had used as a professor. There were people to do many things I previously had to do myself. Someone answered my phone, brought me coffee, made my appointments, and typed my letters. People who hardly spoke to me before suddenly wanted to be my friends. People who had previously ignored me now solicited my opinions. I began to "do lunch" every day. I now even had an expense account to pay for it.

One such lunch was with a dean at another graduate school whom I had known for many years. After our "business" was concluded, he looked at me sorrowfully and said, "You're nuts to have taken this job."

"Why?" I asked anxiously.

"In three years, you'll know why. Not now. Now, you enjoy

the change, the power, the new opportunities. But as time goes on, you'll regret it."

"Why?" I asked again.

"Because," he said, "your career as a scholar is over. The first year, you'll stop writing—no time for that. The second year, you'll stop reading. The third year, you'll stop thinking. Then you'll want to get out and return to scholarship and teaching, but it will be too late."

It's now more than 15 years since that lunch, but I do not regret my decision. The reason is that I took to heart what he said, and I was determined to prove him wrong. And I have. His warning pertained not only to my job but also to any job: A person is always in danger of losing himself by finding a job and then forgetting who he is by becoming submerged in that occupation or profession.

The challenge of work is for it to remain a challenge. When work degenerates into a tedious routine, then it is no longer work but only a job. The goal is to maintain our creativity, to articulate our individual character, and to find meaning and fulfillment in our work. That is the difference between "work" and a "job," a "calling" and a box on an institutional flow chart. The task is not simply to get the job done, but to love what you are doing, even if it is not always lovable. For instance, cleaning up a baby's mess is not lovable, but if it's *your* child, you nonetheless love what you are doing because you love who you are doing it for and why you are doing it. In management, cleaning up other people's messes can be revolting or it can be meaningful. It all depends upon your attitude, upon whether you find meaning in what you are doing, and upon whether you love what you are doing and why you are doing it.

Everyone knows someone who hates going to work. Every morning, thousands of disillusioned workers arrive at work with the sinking feeling that they are wasting another day that cannot be replaced. Studies estimate that the number of such workers has become greater over the past several years and will continue to grow, and that over the long haul, work-related burnout and stress will irreparably damage their physical and mental health. Yet most of us also know people who can hardly wait to get to work in the morning, who are constantly challenged by work, who find great joy and meaning in how they earn their livelihood, who seem nurtured and invigorated by what they do, and for whom money is secondary. Some people look forward to retirement as a "Get Out of Jail Free" card that comes after a long period of incarceration, while others anticipate retirement with dread because it threatens to divest them of the only thing that gave their life meaning.

Which attitude a person embraces may be influenced by the kind of job he has, the type of environment in which he works, the level of compensation he receives, and the expectations he has. In the final analysis, however, a person's attitude toward work is ultimately shaped by who a person is—by his character, values, and sense of meaning and mission. The successful professional can hate what he does while the low-paid laborer can love his work. There is no such thing as menial work—only menial attitudes toward work. The key issue is whether or not work has a purpose or meaning that goes beyond its particular tasks. As the great Russian writer Maxim Gorky wrote, "When work is a pleasure, life is a joy. When work is a duty, life is slavery."

᪣

To relax one night after working many hours on completing a report, I turned on the television set. I began to flip through the channels. On one channel, there was a split screen of what seemed to be bathrooms in an office building. When I looked more closely, I noticed that one was a men's room and one was a ladies' room. In each, a maintenance person was cleaning. Suddenly, there was some music. A title flashed across the screen: "Fundamentals of Management—Session Five, Employee Motivation." A narrator began to speak as the cameras zoomed in on each of the workers washing a bathroom floor.

"Here are two workers on the night shift at an office building in Houston. Their job is to clean all the bathrooms in the building by the time people come to work in the morning. This is not a highly paid or a high prestige job. Theirs is a thankless and tedious job. Yet one of them finds great satisfaction and meaning in her work, while the other hates every minute of it.

Their job is the same, yet their attitude differs. Employee motivation is the key to why some workplaces function better than others. The role of the manager is to be a leader—to provide his employees with a vision of the organization, to motivate with meaning. Motivation makes all the difference. Attitude is the key. Let's see how this works. In this session, we shall discuss the motivation and meaning of work. This is session number five in our on-the-air course 'Fundamentals of Management.' To register for credit, call or write. . . ."

The camera zoomed in further on the woman in the ladies' room, who was now washing the sinks.

"Why do you work here?" the interviewer asks.

"It's a lousy job, but a job. The only job I could get. I hate it—working all night, 7:00 P.M. to 7:00 A.M. The pay stinks, though it's higher because it's the night shift. No one appreciates what I do. I take off sick days whenever I can get away with it. When I have time during the day, I spend it looking for something better. So far, no luck."

The focus now shifted to the second woman, who was scrubbing a urinal in a men's room. She sings while she works. Her enthusiasm is surprising.

"Why do you work here?" the interviewer asks.

She stops washing, stands up, and points to a logo on her uniform. "Do you know what this is?" she asks. "This is the logo of NASA. The workers in this building are all part of NASA. Me, too. I've been working here for eight years. I'm part of a team. In my own way, I'm helping to put an American on Mars. I know it's not much. But I'm doing what I can. Scientists and astronauts use this men's room. I want to be sure everything's clean and tidy for them. I help out in my own way. And one day, when an American astronaut lands on Mars, I'll be able to say that I helped. I did my part. I was part of the team."

☙

People, especially those in low prestige jobs, tend to demean what they do: "I'm only a delivery man," "I just drive a bus," "I'm only a mail carrier." They often fail to see how their job really matters.

In hundreds of interviews reported in his book *Working*, Studs Terkel found examples among American workers of two contrasting attitudes toward work: The first group found meaning, happiness, and fulfillment in their work; the second group experienced drudgery, boredom, and misery. For example, he met an Indiana stonemason who sees a piece of himself in every building he helps to construct, a Chicago piano tuner who seeks and finds sounds that delight, a bookbinder who is gratified to be able to preserve a piece of history, and a Brooklyn fireman who is happy that he is able to save lives. On the other hand, Terkel also spoke to a spot welder who said that he felt like a machine but not treated as well as the machines with which he worked, a bank teller who felt like a prisoner in a cage, a receptionist who said that a monkey could do what she does, and a glamorous fashion model who said that she is an object of people's gazes, not a person.

Life is lived in time, and time is a limited resource that we can spend or invest only once. Time cannot be recycled, replaced, or recaptured. To kill time is murder in the sense that once it's gone, it can never come back. Most of our waking hours, for the majority of our lives, are spent "on the job." The attitude we adopt toward our occupation—toward that which occupies so much of our time—inescapably relates to how we view how our lives are being lived. When we find enjoyment and fulfillment in our work, our lives are replete with happiness and meaning. But when we are dissatisfied with our work, personal satisfaction dwindles and psychic toxins begin to corrode our souls. We may even suffer physically.

What is our real work? Creating our life as a work of art. The challenge is to correlate who we are with what we do, how we occupy our time with how we fulfill our life's mission. The task is to achieve compatibility between our occupation and our work, between how we "make a living" and how we live. For instance, in the 1995 movie *Sabrina*, Harrison Ford plays a businessman whose job has completely taken over his life. At one point, he realizes this and says, "Something is missing from my life—a life."

Whether a person has a paid job or not, everyday living entails work that can make life meaningful. Our daily work includes keeping physically and ethically fit, maintaining our health, and developing our innate talents. To forge and cultivate a friendship, to sustain and deepen a love relationship, and to instruct and nurture a child require unstinting effort.

Tending to things *is* work, whether we are fiscally compensated for it or not. For example, the parent who stays home to raise children has challenging and potentially fulfilling work. The volunteer who donates time and energy to charitable causes has work, but he may have no regular job. The person who gives care and support to a friend or relative who suffers the results of a physical tragedy, such as a stroke, heart attack, or accident, or a psychological trauma, such as the loss of a loved one, takes on a great deal of often difficult and unpleasurable but necessary and meaningful work. Worse than being out of a job is being out of work, because then our lives become devoid of purpose, meaning, and direction. We then float aimlessly through time.

Human nature seems to require us to have purposeful work. People sometimes fantasize about having nothing to do, but psychologists tell us that too much leisure can be dangerous to our health. It can leave us listless, despondent, and disoriented. Even prisoners on death row were found to be happier when they were given work in the prison laundry or kitchen than when they had nothing to do but wait for death. The same seems true of all people. Those without structured and meaningful activity are probable candidates for depression.

Years ago, psychoanalysts wrote about "Sunday neurosis," by which they meant the anxiety and boredom of people with nothing to do on a day of leisure. Indeed, among retired people, finding structured and fulfilling activity can be the difference between health and illness, life and death. Studies show that in the first few years after retirement, heart attack and cancer rates soar, and early death overtakes people who were otherwise healthy before they retired. Already in 1958, the Group for the Advancement of Psychiatry reported that "leisure is a significant danger for many Americans." We apparently need purposeful activity to keep us from becoming bored because the purpose of life is a life of purpose.

How well our job correlates with our life's work determines whether or not "it's just a job." When our job and our life's work are out of sync, then our job satisfaction is sure to decrease, for then we live a double life. We become schizophrenic, leading one life on the job and another off the job. When our job is not part of our work, our lives become split. But when our job is part of our life's work, our lives are integrated and whole.

People express their attitudes toward their jobs by the metaphors they choose to describe their workplace. For instance, dominant metaphors used in the corporate world depict the workplace as a jungle, as a military strike force, or as a football team. The competition becomes an enemy to be attacked and defeated. The motto evoked is Vince Lombardi's statement that "winning isn't everything, it's the only thing."

Who is the enemy against whom we are competing? Who are we out to defeat? Not only the companies that compete with our own, but also our own co-workers—those below us on the corporate ladder who bite at our heels like jackals waiting to take us down and replace us, and those above us on the organizational chart who are trying to push us out before we can replace them. In such an environment, a person lives on adrenaline with fight-or-flight instincts on constant full alert, a nervous wreck, riddled with anxiety, debilitated by stress, nurtured by Maalox.

Is it just chance that more heart attacks occur on Monday between 8:00 and 9:00 A.M. than at any other time during the week? Physician Larry Dossey thinks that this is not accidental. Rather, Dr. Dossey believes that this is because people dread going to jobs that offer low meaning and high stress. Joyless, meaningless, stressful work is, according to Dr. Dossey, at least as great a factor in heart disease as high cholesterol and smoking. Further, a report of the United Nations International Labor Organization labels job stress as "one of the most serious health issues of the twentieth century."

When the world of work is characterized by relentless stress and anxiety, when it is seen as a world at war, everyone becomes a potential casualty. Work as war turns everyone into a warrior. Work in a jungle turns everyone into a beast. To see the goal of work or the goal of life as being a survivor or "winner" is to view others as threats or adversaries. For us to win, they have to lose. Their failure is necessary for our success. Can there be loyalty, camaraderie, honesty, care, creativity, or cooperation in such an environment? When the goal becomes winning at all costs, other concerns fall by the wayside. Often in such an environment, everybody loses out.

Creating life as a work of art aims at individual excellence, not competitive excellence. In the art of soul-crafting, the goal is not to be the best, but to be the best you can be, to compete against yourself rather than against others. As the great ballet dancer Mikhail Baryshnikov once said, "I do not try to dance better than anyone else. I only try to dance better than myself." In making decisions, the key question is, will this choice help me to become the person that I want to be, that I hope to become? The aim is not victory over someone else, but the improvement of one's own self.

A young man once came to see me with his father, who is a friend of mine. The son is a graduate of an Ivy League college and of a leading law school. After practicing law for a few years in a prominent law firm, he left everything to live in a Buddhist monastery. The last time I had seen him, he was dressed in a three-piece suit, his hair styled, his shoes shined. Now, he sat before me with a shaven head, wrapped in an orange robe with sandals on his feet.

"Why did you do it?" I asked him.

"I was tired of the competition, the pressure, the dog-eat-dog world. All I did at the law firm was try to upstage the other associates so that I could become a partner before they did."

"And now?" I asked. "How is life in the monastery?"

"It's wonderful," he said. "It's the fulfillment of my life's meaning. All day I do all the legal work for the monastery. I started there as the master's most lowly disciple, but in a very short time I've worked my way up to #3 disciple."

⁓⊃

A workplace in which "the law of the jungle" has replaced moral virtues such as loyalty, honesty, and truthfulness cannot be either productive or efficient in the long run. In a workplace where the ruthless rule, the creativity needed for effective productivity falls by the wayside. Energy that could be invested in collaborative efforts is dissipated by constant fear, paranoia, and stress. Backbiting competitive aggression stifles the potential to achieve individual excellence and to advance the common good.

For many, the workplace continues to be a combat zone. For increasing numbers of workers, however, the workplace is becoming their new neighborhood, their new extended family. With the dissolution of local neighborhoods, with families geographically scattered as never before, and with more people living alone than in previous generations, the workplace is increasingly becoming the source of friendships, social activities, and personal support.

People who can apply what they learn in the workplace to the rest of their lives, and vice versa, are fortunate. For example, a person who learns how to transform anger and disappointment toward a co-worker into a constructive and cooperative working relationship can apply those skills when in the midst of an argument with his or her spouse. An individual who develops problem-solving abilities can apply them in a moment of personal crisis. The skills needed to achieve objectives through teamwork on the job can be transferred anywhere from the family to the civic arena. When there is a synergy between what we do on and off the job, both job satisfaction and life satisfaction are bound to improve. But when the workday is spent as an animal in a jungle, as a commando on a battlefield, it is unlikely that crossing the threshold between the office and the home will magically transform someone from a predator to a caring and nurturing human being.

When a person perceives the workplace as a battleground or as a jungle, there can be little promise of job satisfaction—unless, of course, that person sees himself primarily as a warrior or as a predator. In other words, not only how a person perceives the workplace but also how he sees himself are critical components of how his occupational attitudes are shaped.

Since the Industrial Revolution, the machine has dominated our way of thinking. The resulting mechanistic view of human beings and of the universe has its roots in early-modern philosophy and physics. For example, the seventeenth-century French philosopher Julien Offray de La Mettrie wrote an influential book called *Man, a Machine.* In this book, La Mettrie asks, How is the human machine different from other machines? His answer: Only the human machine winds its own springs.

This view of the human being as a machine has become deeply embedded in our mentality. It affects our views of others, our world, our work, and ourselves. For example, in our daily colloquial speech, we tend to speak of ourselves as if we are machines. We are "turned on" or "turned off." We "tune in" and "tune out." We "gear up" and "wind down." We "recharge our batteries." We provide "input" and "output." Even the model for the doctor/patient relationship in our country conceives of the human being as a machine in need of occasional repair, rather than as a person who requires caring and curing. Ours is a civilization of machines, said the Nobel Prize–winning French author André Malraux, and machines can teach a human being everything except how to be a human being.

Most businesses, most workplaces, are corporations. The English word *corporation* comes from the Latin word *corpus*, which means "a body." The task of the worker is to provide that body with a soul. The Greek word for soul is *anima*, from which the English word *animate* derives. People at work are there to animate the workplace, to give it life, soul, and purpose. Animation cannot be provided by a soulless machine or by a machinelike person. It can only come from a soulful and creative human being.

With the Industrial Revolution, we became machines running other machines. Machinelike labor reduced the worker to a cog in a machine. Mechanical work became the paradigm for the alienation of the worker from his work. This was satirized brilliantly by Charlie Chaplin in his classic film *Modern Times* (1936), where Charlie's work in a mammoth industrial plant is to tighten one bolt on an endless assembly line. Every decade since that film was made serves to confirm its lesson—that it is dangerous to depersonalize workers by transforming them into extensions of the machines with which they work, whether it's on an assembly line or with a computer. Machinelike labor brings alienation, tedium, and a feeling of isolation. Such labor inevitably becomes boring, and boredom is the enemy of meaning and creativity.

When work becomes boring, depression fills the void. When work becomes meaningless, despair sets in. It is well-documented that such feelings weaken the immune system and invite the onset of a variety of diseases. We also know that purpose, hope, and appreciation bolster the immune system and enhance both our physical and spiritual health. The great Russian novelist Dostoyevsky reminded us that "to annihilate a person completely, give him work of an absolutely useless and irrational nature."

Work is effort applied to a purpose, and the ideal state for work as for life has been called flow. Flow is the application of one's knowledge and skills to a purpose at hand. If the challenge exceeds the skills, frustration will ensue. If skills exceed the challenge, boredom will result. But if the challenge correlates with the skills, the person's attention becomes focused upon the purpose of the activity. Though people perform at their peak while in flow, they are paradoxically unconcerned with how they are doing while they are doing it. They are motivated by the sheer pleasure of the activity and utterly absorbed in what they are doing. In such moments, the person is egoless, devoid of self-consciousness. Yet simultaneously, the self is enlarged, enhanced, and enriched. Anxiety dissolves while efficient skills are applied to the task at hand. There is joy simply in the doing. Motivations of reward or validation by others become irrelevant. The activity itself becomes intrinsically rewarding. Work becomes a labor of love. Work, like a lover, is loved for its own sake. There is value, virtue, joy, and fulfillment in the act of work as in the act of love.

When a person feels in control of what he is doing, he feels less stress. Indeed, a major cause of stress is the feeling of having little control over one's situation. For example, a study of British civil service workers found that those who experienced the highest incidents of disease from work-related stress were those who believed themselves to have little or no control over their assigned tasks. In a mechanical environment, workers feel like cogs in a wheel, easily dispensable, readily replaceable, part of a machine that operates beyond their control, with or without them. In a creative work environment, people feel ownership for what they do. They can point proudly to their personal contribution to a product or a service provided.

When we see ourselves as artists rather than as machines, as creative beings rather than as mechanisms, the promise of creating life as an art form becomes possible. Finding meaning and purpose in our work becomes realizable. It is not coincidental that psychologist Mihaly Csikszentmihalyi formulated the idea of flow when he was studying how artists work. There are four ways of achieving flow, according to Csikszentmihalyi, professor at the University of Chicago and author of numerous books, including the bestseller *Flow*. They are:

> Set goals.
> Immerse yourself in the activity.
> Pay attention to what is happening; be aware.
> Enjoy the immediacy of the experience.

Like the meaning of one's life, sometimes the meaning of one's work takes many years of study, training, discipline, and effort until it becomes apparent. Recognition and reward often take time. But for a person in flow it doesn't really matter. For instance, in a study of art students, Csikszentmihalyi discovered that those who savored the sheer joy of painting were more likely to become serious and successful painters than were those who were motivated in school by dreams of fame and fortune. The artist who painted while thinking of how the critics would review his work and of what sales price he would ask was less likely to achieve creative heights than the artist who was single-mindedly immersed in the act of painting itself.

The hope of being remembered is a motivating factor that provides meaning in one's work not only for the artist but for other workers as well. Commenting on the workers he interviewed, Terkel writes, "Perhaps immortality, too, is part of the quest. To be remembered was the wish, spoken or unspoken, of the heroes and heroines of this book." As the great American pragmatic philosopher William James once wrote, "The greatest use of life is to spend it for something that will outlast it." Our life's work is to create something of ourselves, from ourselves, that can transcend and survive this life. In the creation of each of our lives as works of art, we would be wise to be guided by Robert Browning's poetic admonition: "Reach should exceed grasp, else what's a Heaven for?"

Once there was a young man who wanted to become a blacksmith. So he became an apprentice to a master blacksmith, and he learned all the necessary techniques of the trade: how to hold the tongs, how to lift the sledge, how to smite the anvil, even how to blow the fire with the bellows. Having completed his apprenticeship, he was chosen to be employed at the smithy of the royal palace. The young man's delight soon came to an end, however, when he discovered that he had failed to learn how to kindle the spark. All his skill and knowledge in handling the tools were to no avail. Meaningful work begins with knowing how to kindle the spark within one's own self.

✎ 14 ✎

The Pursuit of Happiness

Do not all human beings desire happiness? . . .
What human being is there who does not desire happiness?

—Plato

*B*ecause I have taught Kabbalah, or Jewish mysticism, for many years, I receive many phone calls and letters that most people would find unusual. It takes each new secretary that I have worked with considerable time to get used to these inquiries. For example, there was the convicted murderer in a maximum security prison who wanted me to exorcise the evil from him so that he wouldn't kill again. Once a woman wanted to share the mysteries of the universe with me that she claimed were revealed to her when she was abducted by aliens. Another time a gym teacher demanded that I remove a curse put on him by his girlfriend's former lover that caused his genitals to shrink. I had a call from a woman who told me that she collected numbers that she saw in visions, which she was able to use to predict the future. Furthermore, there was the lady who invited me over to her house to speak to the ghosts that she believed were constantly rearranging her furniture.

Once in the middle of one of my classes, a student took ill and got up to leave. Another student ran after him, claiming that she was a faith healer who could cure him by placing her hands on his body.

"Put your hands on your head and cure yourself," he said, and left the room.

So when I received a phone call one day from my friend June who told me that she wanted to come to talk to me about why she was unhappy, I was somewhat relieved.

A few days after June called, we met to discuss why she wasn't happy. I hoped to apply what I had learned from a lifetime of study to June's problem, a problem that plagues many people: how to attain genuine meaning, goodness, and happiness in life. Clearly, the insights and wisdom of past generations have much to say about the complexities of the present.

Unlike many others, June was not embarrassed to admit that she wasn't happy. Instead, she was startled that her life was not characterized by the deepest and most abiding happiness. Simply put, she had it all. June was in her late thirties. She was unusually beautiful, very wealthy, in wonderful physical health, and professionally accomplished. She had an adoring husband with a lucrative law practice, three adorable children, and an active social life where she easily mingled with the rich and the famous. She had much more than most, and less than few. Yet she felt a hollowness in her life. There was no reason why she shouldn't be happy—or so she thought.

Like so many other people frustrated by the lack of contentment in their lives, June had tried a whole menu of methods aimed at capturing the elusive bliss. She had attended workshops in personal growth, but she still felt spiritually stunted. After spending many hours in motivational seminars, she continued to find herself looking for a reason to get out of bed. She had participated in a wide variety of programs offered by self-proclaimed gurus, psychologists, and psychiatrists—from tai chi to Rolfing. But her innermost self still cried out for help and happiness. Having labored to get in touch with her feelings, she still wondered why passion remained so elusive. Having climbed the 12 steps toward recovery and health, she still had to overcome the onset of anxiety and malaise. Having healed her "inner child," she still faced the task of creating a life of fulfillment, beauty, and happiness for her inner adult. And even if she found her "true self," she still would have to ask herself what to do with it once it was found. June, who seemed to have all the ingredients for a life of happiness and meaning, failed to attain it because she was looking in the wrong places. Rather than focusing on her abilities—rather than creating her life as a work of art—she had concentrated on her alleged illnesses and syndromes. June's predicament reminded me of something a CEO of a large corporation once said to me, paraphrasing the Bible: "Man cannot live on Prozac alone."

Ours has become a pathological society where people define themselves by the diseases, syndromes, and dysfunctions that afflict them. People not only have diseases and syndromes—real and imagined—but they tend to make that fact an integral feature of their personal identities. "Hi, I'm Jim, a diabetic." "Hi, I'm Jane and I'm recovering from a self-defeating personality syndrome." The malady has the person as much as the person has the malady. This pathological approach to health and to identity tends to carry over into how we see the world. What's bad in society—the tragedies that occur daily, the social and economic problems afflicting our society—are what we usually hear about. The social focus is on disease, pathology, and dysfunction—not upon happiness, meaning, joy, or creativity.

When we equate health with happiness, people are led to believe that if they are not happy, it must be because they are sick. A popular tactic of social and psychiatric workers, also known as the "helping professionals," has been to try to convince people that they are victims of some illness or syndrome and that's why they aren't happy. The applied logic then becomes that since they're victims, they aren't responsible for their own unhappiness. Someone or something outside of themselves caused it. Consequently, to arrive at the door of happiness, they must first traverse the never-ending path toward health. The promise is that once they're healthy, they'll be happy.

If people are told often enough that they are sick and dysfunctional, that they are unwilling victims not only of viruses and bacteria but also of disorders, syndromes, and a host of "isms," it will eventually make them depressed. And we know for sure that depression is not conducive to health or happiness. Among its other results, depression weakens the immune system. The fear of our physical and psychological health being compromised by external factors has led many to adopt a "siege mentality" where opportunities for moral development, spiritual self-expression, and happiness are stifled by the paranoia of self-protection. While it would be naive not to be aware of potential and actual dangers, it may be counterproductive to be primarily motivated by that which we fear, rather than by that which we find meaningful, valuable, and enjoyable.

True, lasting, and genuine happiness entails being good. The moral virtues are directional signals that mark the way toward bliss, fulfillment, and the meaning and mission of human existence. Moral virtues are the foundation upon which we construct our character and fashion a purposeful, fulfilled, and happy life. Cultivating the moral virtues requires taking a proactive rather than a reactive role in the creation of one's life as a work of art.

I checked into a hotel in Europe not long ago. A sign over the desk said: "For your protection, please leave your values at the front desk." A bad translation from English, but an accurate description of a current trend.

When a Harvard professor asked his students who was responsible for the Holocaust, some of them took the "no fault" view of history—that events like the Holocaust "just happen," like a random, reckless occurrence. Other students quoted recent studies that claim Hitler's actions were the result of his having been abused by his father. Hence, Hitler was really a victim rather than a victimizer, and consequently not responsible for hurling the world into chaos. Furthermore, this view contends that as a victim of abuse, Hitler should receive our compassion rather than our contempt!

If genocide can occur with no one being responsible, then how can we expect people to be held responsible for less hideous deeds? How can we expect anyone to be held responsible for anything?

Most criminal lawyers know the famous "Twinkie defense." In a murder case, the defendant pleaded not guilty, denying responsibility for a murder he admitted to committing. When asked why he should not be held responsible for this murder, the defendant said that he didn't really mean to kill anybody, but when he eats too many Twinkies, he loses control and goes on a murderous rampage. Whose fault is it? Who then is responsible for the murdering of his innocent victim?

The defense attorney claimed that the responsibility was certainly not that of the defendant. Rather, Twinkies were responsible because they are addictive—like a narcotic. The attorney suggested that perhaps Twinkies should be sold only with a doctor's prescription. Further, the defense argued that though this addiction is normally not harmful, it is especially harmful to people with diabetes because it causes an imbalance in their endocrine system, and when they experience this imbalance, they cannot control their actions or be responsible for them. As it happened, this murderer was a diabetic with a Twinkies addiction—which was not his own fault, but his mother's because she fed him Twinkies as a child.

Imagine Cain mounting the Twinkies defense after killing Abel. Instead of saying, "Am I my brother's keeper?" he might say, "Yes, I killed Abel, but I'm not guilty. It's all because Eve fed me too many figs. I'm just a fig addict. When I eat too many figs, I lose control of myself. That's why I killed Abel. It's not my fault."

A few years ago, a sociologist conducted a survey to determine what percentage of the American population considers itself a member of an oppressed minority group. The sociologist tallied his findings, expecting the results to be about 20 percent at the highest. But when the final results were counted up, he was surprised at the result: The majority of the U.S. population considers itself members of oppressed minority groups. Hence, we now have the strange situation where it is becoming increasingly fashionable and desirable to be a victim.

The Americans with Disabilities Act was passed to try to end discrimination against people with handicaps, such as blindness and deafness. People with disabilities were to be given a chance to use the abilities that they do have. But because of the special privileges and considerations available under the Americans with Disabilities Act, it is becoming increasingly fashionable and desirable to identify a disability that one might have. Now people want to be victims of some disability that would give them special attention or some way of escaping from responsibility.

Some examples:

A 400-pound woman sues McDonald's for "size discrimination" because she cannot sit in the chairs provided at their restaurants. It does not occur to her that maybe she should go on a diet.

A man with an affinity for gambling with other people's money is fired from his job. Later he is reinstated after a court rules that his compulsive gambling is a "handicap" and is protected by the Americans with Disabilities Act. Rather than going to jail, he continues to enjoy his "handicap," at the expense of others.

Fired from his job because he consistently shows up late for work, an employee successfully sues for reinstatement on the grounds that he has been discriminated against because of a personality disorder that afflicts him. The disorder is "Chronic Lateness Syndrome." It doesn't occur to him that maybe he needs an alarm clock.

"Syndromes," like "Chronic Lateness Syndrome," are listed in the *Diagnostical and Statistical Manual of Mental Disorders* (D.S.M.) put out by the American Psychiatric Association. Here many types of behavior that we would characterize either as inappropriate or immoral are diagnosed as sicknesses. This diagnosis then limits the responsibility of persons who manifest such behavior, possibly qualifying them for health insurance payments to be treated for it and potentially protecting them under the legal shield of the Americans with Disabilities Act.

If you think I'm exaggerating, consider the following: A young woman in New Jersey was attending her senior prom in 1997. She was in the ninth month of a pregnancy. She was not married. While at the prom, she went into labor. She went to the ladies' room, delivered the baby herself, apparently smothered it to death, threw it in the garbage, and returned to the prom to dance. Some of the psychotherapists who later examined her diagnosed her as suffering from a syndrome listed in the D.S.M.: "brief psychotic disorder with postpartum onset." Should she be held responsible for what she did?

It is ironic that in American society, which has traditionally cherished individualism and self-initiative, this "therapeutic" approach has largely succeeded in disenfranchising us of independence and responsibility in order to make us dependent upon others for virtually every aspect of our daily existence. This stifles us from initiating our own spiritual journeys toward happiness and goodness. It creates dependency on others to accomplish tasks that would otherwise be our personal responsibility.

The therapeutic approach encourages us to organize our lives around our wounds, maladies, and syndromes, rather than around our life's meaning, our spiritual development, and our ability to create our lives as works of art. Spiritual development is often mistakenly equated with healing. But they are not identical. Healing is restorative, therapeutic. Spiritual and moral development is creative, dynamic. The crafting of life as a work of art challenges us with becoming practitioners of evolution rather than victims of evolution and environment.

The waiting rooms at psychiatrists' offices are filled with people who have achieved substantial financial and professional success, but who wonder why the symbols of happiness they have acquired, like money and social status, have not brought them the happiness, contentment, meaning, and self-fulfillment they seek. Such people keep believing that if they had even more money, if they were in better physical shape, if they were celebrities, they would be truly happy. But what they fail to realize is that the quest for success is a treadmill that never stops and that there comes a time when it is necessary to step off the treadmill and to think about where one is going and about what one expects to find when one gets there.

People tend to forget that financial or professional success is only one kind of success, and that's why it cannot guarantee either complete success or lasting happiness. A person can be successful professionally while being a failure as a parent, a spouse, a colleague, or a friend. The most successful businessperson can be an abysmal failure as a human being. Success as a human being is achieved by cultivating the moral virtues. Albert Einstein once advised, "Try not to be a man of success, but try to become a man of virtue."

When success becomes the purpose of existence, everything else becomes a means to that end—family, career, friendships. In his enormously popular book *The Power of Positive Thinking*, the Reverend Norman Vincent Peale recommended belief in God and prayer as a means of increasing our ability to be successful. For Reverend Peale, even God should be subordinated to the god of success. But what Reverend Peale seems to have forgotten is that his own Protestant tradition has a name for subordinating God to anything—"idolatry."

When success becomes an end in itself, it is unlikely that it can serve as a means to happiness—or to anything else. Even if success can serve as an ingredient in happiness, it is only one of many ingredients needed. And if success has been purchased at the price of having sacrificed all the other elements, enduring happiness will continue to elude us. Furthermore, as we have seen in chapter 10, what is true of success is also true of the acquisition of money. When it begins as a means to an end and then becomes an end in itself, the original goal grows ever more elusive. Just as having more success does not guarantee being happier, having more money is no guarantor of increased happiness.

Animals seem content when their biological needs are met. Human beings require something more. When their basic needs are met, human beings often create new needs, and if those are met, there are then more new needs. This becomes an unending spiral that never leads to true happiness or fulfillment. Eventually, one is drawn to inquire: Now that my needs are met, am *I* needed? Who needs *me*? What is the purpose of my being in this world? The real question, says Rabbi Harold Kushner, is not "How far will I go?" but "When it's over, what will my life have been about?"

Some people believe that fame will ensure happiness, but the testimony of those who have been there is not what we might expect. For example, at the height of his career, comedian Eddie Murphy posed the question asked by many well-known people: "Now I'm famous. How come I'm not happy all the time?" Similarly, shortly before her death in a car crash, TV anchorwoman Jessica Savitch said, "My life's never been more of a mess, and I've never been more popular."

᭞

Once I went to an exclusive private club for a business lunch. I was waiting to be seated when in walked an ex-Congressman who had frequented the club for many years. He had only recently been voted out of office. He asked for his "usual table." The maître d' told him that it was unavailable, even though he saw it was unoccupied. "Don't you know who I am?" he railed. The maître d' replied, "No, but I know who you were."

᭞

When fleeting fame comes to an end, when the beauty of the famous actress fades, when the reflexes of the great athlete slow down, when the powerful politician is out of the public eye, when the business magnate is downsized, what is left? Who is left?

Physical pleasure is an important component of life, but can it ensure happiness? If eating food were not pleasurable, we might die of starvation. If sex were not pleasurable, our species might now be extinct. Without physical pleasure, life would be a bland, colorless, and monotonous pastime. Pleasure is the spice of life. Yet pleasure simply for the sake of pleasure often ends up demonstrating that always doing what feels good can easily lead to feeling bad. For instance, rats that have a choice between eating and electrically stimulating the pleasure centers of their brains will choose stimulation and will die of hunger—and of pleasure. Similar human behavior shows how easily we, too, can succumb to physical pleasure. Pleasure as an end in itself is a dead end. It offers pleasing physical sensations but not happiness.

One of the purposes of pleasure is to stimulate awareness, to heighten consciousness. For example, standing on the top of Aspen Mountain in Colorado and seeing the Rocky Mountains all around you will heighten your awareness of the wonder and mystery of nature. Sexual pleasure can increase the bond within the relationship. It can serve as a way of expressing what transcends words. It can literally "make love." It can make one aware of the gift that is giving. Yet the most creative acts, the most fulfilling experiences, the accomplishments that offer the most profound and durable happiness are often those that are not necessarily associated only with physical pleasure. For instance, the athlete who strives for excellence must exercise extreme physical and mental discipline and often must endure pain to expand his physical capabilities. The literary or visual artist must often contend with anguish, anxiety, and the trying acquisition of difficult skills to produce a work of art. The scientist may experience intense frustration in the process of experimentation that might one day lead to a new discovery. Pleasure is no guarantor of happiness. It may serve as a stimulus, but it cannot serve as an end in itself. The most tragic example of this phenomenon in our society is drugs. The drug culture is an expression of the confusion of pleasure with happiness.

Pleasure alone cannot produce abiding happiness. Something more is required. But what? What is this happiness that we seek, that we pursue? Helen Keller answered this question by saying, "Many persons have a wrong idea of what constitutes true happiness. It is not attained through self-gratification but through fidelity to a worthy purpose." This view echoes those of ancient philosophers as well as contemporary psychologists.

Recent psychological studies show that people absorbed in the pursuit of pleasure for pleasure's sake, who prefer long-term unstructured leisure over purposeful activity, who passively and constantly consume commercially produced entertainment rather than engage in creative and meaningful activities, tend to be bored and depressed more often than not. These studies also show that meeting challenging goals, achieving one's purposes—despite the obstacles that must be overcome to do so—being disciplined despite the physical inconvenience it may cause, and working toward completing the tasks we have assigned for ourselves is the path toward meaning, fulfillment, and durable happiness. The questions used to be: How do I overcome the maladies, syndromes, and disabilities that have victimized me? The questions now are: What are our minimum daily requirements for spiritual development, and where and how do we locate them? How can I create my life as a work of art?

To a person grounded in the teachings of the great religious and philosophical traditions of the past, most of the teachings of this "new" trend are remarkably familiar. They are not new at all. Rather, they merely seem to translate into a contemporary idiom observations and teachings that have been known and cultivated by philosophical and religious teachings for many generations. The recent "discovery" of the soul, of the spiritual, is really a rediscovery of what has preoccupied cartographers of the spiritual and moral journey for thousands of years.

The simple word *flow* is increasingly used today to depict this phenomenon of deep personal satisfaction and happiness. In past generations, similar states were known by a variety of other names, such as "ecstasy" and "transcendence." It entails commitment to a challenging task—applying all of one's energy, knowledge, and experience toward completing the task, and, hopefully, reaching one's desired goal. Boredom, depression, and chaos are defeated as the person achieves a sense of exhilaration that comes when his purposes have been attained.

In flow, a goal becomes wedded to a specific task. This entails the focusing of attention on a clearly defined goal; the person knows what must be done and how to do it. Irrelevant stimuli and

thoughts are excluded from the person's immediate awareness;
the "static" is filtered out so that the person can concentrate on
the task at hand. A merging of action and awareness should then
ensue. The actor and the action become one. Already attained
skills are applied without self-consciousness, without thought of
external rewards. Ironically, when a person is caught up in the
flow, he does not feel himself in control, yet he finds himself able
to exercise control over remarkably complex and difficult situations. Acquired discipline and knowledge merge with spontaneous action in the pursuit of the focused goal. An individual becomes absorbed in the activity for its own sake. He becomes lost
in the activity, too busy to think of himself, too involved in the
task to be self-conscious. Paradoxically, though self-concern dis-
appears during the activity, the sense of self emerges stronger
after the experience.

Like music, a flow activity is partly scored and partly impro-
vised. We have control, yet we also lose control. Our acuity is at
its sharpest. The realm of our senses is heightened. We look at
the same things, yet we are able to see more than before. We
listen to the same sounds, yet we hear them in a new, amplified,
and enriched manner. Our sense of touch conveys a broadened
sense of awareness. Our sense of smell becomes surprisingly
heightened. Our sense of timing becomes remarkably synchronic.
We become in tune with what we are doing, with who we are,
with who we want to become. We experience the present in all
its fullness. We taste the whole kernel of the moment before it is
ground into powder by the imposition of external analysis, measurement, judgment, or approval. The boundaries of the self are
expanded, voids within the soul are suddenly filled, and ego
boundaries seem erased as the individual transcends his own self.
Chaos is cheated as we fulfill our sense of purpose. And, ultimately, it all depends on first having faith in a transcendent system
of meaning that offers coherence and purpose to life.

As a result of such an experience, we find out something new
about ourselves; we both transcend and transform ourselves. We
become more than we were, more of who we want to become.
In this way, everyday experiences can become elevated experi-

ences. Theologians call this the sanctification of the mundane, the hallowing of those experiences that constitute our daily routine. Flow can transform the mundane into the sacred, the routine into the enjoyable, the tedious into the transcendent. Such an experience is also enjoyable and autotelic, that is, worth seeking for its own intrinsic (rather than extrinsic or societal) rewards and fulfillment. Such a feeling of accomplishment and approval comes from within rather than from without.

In ancient and medieval philosophy, there is an idea similar to flow. This view links true and lasting happiness to the human being's ability to realize his potential, to fulfill his goals, to actualize the purpose of his life. Unlike the contemporary idea of flow which can relate to any activity, however, these ancient and medieval thinkers focused upon those particular activities that directly relate to qualities and activities that make us uniquely human. In their view, enduring happiness is achieved by fulfilling our human mission to create life as a work of art through the cultivation of the moral virtues, through making virtuous living a habit. For Aristotle, and for many of the medievals who embraced his teachings, being good is the answer to four important questions.

> How do I carry out the mission of human existence?
> How do I create for myself an excellent life?
> How can I develop those potentials buried within myself that are sometimes obscured even from my own vision?
> How do I achieve a form of happiness that can endure?

Once a woman dreamed that she walked into a store and found God standing behind the counter. God said to her, "You can have anything your heart desires, just wish for it."

"I want happiness, love, and wisdom," said the woman.

God looked at her and said, "I don't think you understand. I can give you only seeds. Whether they become flowers is up to you."

Some Further Reading

When I was a very young boy, my grandmother told me to make books my friends. Through books, she said, I could discover many things beyond the orbit of my own experience. I could meet the wisest people who ever lived and absorb some of their wisdom. I could immeasurably enrich my own life by earning what others throughout the world and in centuries past and present had learned about the great adventure of living. Since then, books have been my constant companions, accompanying me everywhere I go. Like good friends, I choose them carefully. Like faithful friends, they do not desert me. They generously share their knowledge with me.

In writing this book, I have drawn upon my own life experience, for as the poet Walt Whitman said, in the person we find the universal. I hope that some of the episodes that I have shared with you from my own life resonate with some of those from your own life. I hope this book provides some insight about how to create into a beautiful work of art your own life, the lives of those whom you love, and the lives of those who love you. Yet, this book would not have been possible had I not consulted with many of my friends, including books I have read and studied over the years, both by authors now living and by authors who flourished centuries ago. I hope that this book has become your friend and that you will permit it to introduce you to some of its friends who are my companions as well.

↬ *The Book of Virtues* by William Bennett

↬ *The Conquest of Happiness* by Bertrand Russell

↬ *Critique of Practical Reason* by Immanuel Kant

↬ *Emotional Intelligence* by Daniel Goleman

↬ *The Ethics of Authenticity* by Charles Taylor

↬ *Ethics of the Fathers* (in the Talmud)

↬ *Flow: The Psychology of Optimal Experience* by Mihaly Csik-szentmihalyi

↬ *The Gift of Peace* by Joseph Cardinal Bernardin

↬ *Holy Scriptures*

↬ *How Good Do We Have to Be?* by Harold Kushner

↬ *How Good People Make Choices* by Rushworth Kidder

↬ *Markings* by Dag Hammarskjöld

↬ *A Nation of Victims: The Decay of the American Character* by Charles J. Sykes

↬ *The Nature of Creativity* by Robert J. Sternberg

↬ *Nicomachean Ethics* by Aristotle

↬ *The Pursuit of Happiness* by David G. Myers

↬ *The Pursuit of Love* by Irving Singer

↬ *The Reinvention of Work* by Matthew Fox

↬ *The Seven Deadly Sins* by Solomon Schimmel

↬ *Teach Yourself Ethics* by Mel Thompson

↬ *Thoughts on Virtue*

↬ *To Love and Be Loved* by Sam Keen

↬ *Utilitarianism* by John Stuart Mill

↬ *Who Is Man?* by Abraham Joshua Heschel

↬ *Words That Hurt, Words That Heal* by Joseph Telushkin

↬ *Working* by Studs Terkel

Why Be Good? has not only friends but also siblings, which are the more than twenty other books I have written. Like siblings in a family, some of them resemble *Why Be Good?* but have their own nature and personality. Three of them are *Crafting the Soul: Creating Your Life as a Work of Art*, *Thank God: Prayers of Jews and Christians Together* (written with Sr. Carol Frances Jegen), and *How to Be a Jew: Ethical Teachings of Judaism* (written with Rabbi Seymour J. Cohen).

Index